ROAD *grill*

WITH
MATT DUNIGAN
CHRIS KNIGHT

McArthur & Company
Toronto

First published in 2008 by
McArthur & Company
322 King St. West, Suite 402
Toronto, ON
M5V 1J2
www.mcarthur-co.com

Library and Archives Canada Cataloguing in Publication

    Knight, Chris, 1960-   Road grill / Chris Knight.

    ISBN 978-1-55278-703-8

    1. Barbecue cookery. I. Title.
    TX840.B3K555 2008   641.7'6   C2008-901594-0

Design and composition by *Mad Dog Design Connection*
Printed in Canada by *Transcontinental*

"The Simpsons" quote from "Lisa the Vegetarian" episode 133 ™ and © FOX.

All Photos Courtesy Knight Enterprises Copyright 2007
Photographer: *Vanessa Poirier-Ogg*

The publisher would like to acknowledge the financial support of the Government of Canada through the Book Publishing Industry Development Program (BPIDP) and the Canada Council for our publishing activities. The publisher further wishes to acknowledge the financial support of the Ontario Arts Council for our publishing program.

10 9 8 7 6 5 4 3 2 1

To my best friend Adam
who makes it all worthwhile.

CONTENTS

Foreword

Wow, who knew? Ten to twelve hours of shooting for twenty-two minutes of television. Filming an episode of *Road Grill* was definitely a full day's work (if you can call it that), the kind of work that makes you pinch yourself to make sure you're not dreaming.

Little did I know that night in January, 2007, when my beautiful wife Kathy and I shot an amateur audition video (after a few cocktails), that I would actually be hosting a TV show. The audition tape was for Knight Enterprises' nationwide casting call for the next Grilling Guru. I planned to show them just how much I knew about grilling and overwhelm them with my on-camera presence. Well, that didn't happen.

But what did happen was simply extraordinary. Some may call it the luck of the Irish, my brother Scott would tell me I live a charmed life; whatever the reason, I was fortunate enough to be invited to put together a real audition tape for the wonderful folks at Food Network Canada to give them a better glimpse of who I really am. I'm not sure if that was a good thing, but I can tell you that once I was in the middle of shooting that second audition tape I knew Chris Knight's vision was something very special. Chris surrounded himself with extremely talented and passionate people so I knew that this was going to be good – very good – not to mention a ton of fun.

Well, Scott was right. The stars aligned and the seas parted and sure enough here I am – the host of the new Knight Enterprises production called *Road Grill*.

Welcome to all things BBQ. Kerry Galvin, Jenna Durling, Charlotte Langley and I travel the country looking for people having a good time enjoying the outdoors and opportunities to cook up some awesome recipes on the grill. Sounds fun, doesn't it? Well it's a blast and I'm having the time of my life hosting this show. I'm constantly learning all kinds of new things – especially about the variety of delicious foods you can cook up on the BBQ.

Hey, here's the deal. I want you to take a big breath and jump in, just like I had to this past year when I took the chance to reinvent myself and learn more about a whole new world. The *Road Grill* cookbook will help you transform your BBQ experience into something far beyond your wildest dreams.

Enjoy!

Matt Dunigan

Introduction

And God said, "Let there be fire"
And Man said, "Let there be BBQ"
And it was good.

The book of Bubba, 10:10

Welcome to the *Road Grill* cookbook, a celebration of all things BBQ. There are many good barbecue books out there and we thank you for choosing ours. We hope it brings BBQ joy and pleasure for years to come.

In order to differentiate ourselves from those other books, we have brought our considerable resources to bear on researching the history and evolution of BBQ. It is generally held that BBQ can trace its origins to that time when Spanish galleons first landed in the Caribbean, and that "barbecue" comes from an ancient aboriginal Haitian word meaning "a wooden structure upon which to sleep or cure meat," hopefully not at the same time. Sparing no expense, our team has discovered that the origins of barbecue are considerably older than that. In fact barbecue is more than two million years old. We, the people of *Road Grill*, now share with you a truth so staggering, so revolutionary, that it just might change your life forever. Ready? Here goes:

1 **The very evolution of Mankind and every milestone, every moment of inspired creativity, every invention, everything that we know and hold dear along that evolutionary path . . . is directly attributable to BBQ, and . . .**

2 **BBQ was invented by a woman.**

Pretty earth-shattering, isn't it? Bold statements, you say? Allow me to explain.

First let us consider the issue of who invented BBQ. I'm pretty sure it was a woman. This is of course a controversial statement given men, even culinarily-challenged men, consider BBQ to be "guys' work." For the most part, women are quite happy to let this stereotype slide, as they do most of the cooking anyway. Barbecues are one of the few household "appliances" specifically marketed to the man of the house – manufactured in jet black or British racing green with lots of chrome and steel. Come summer, a man's measure is the size of his grill surface. Do not ever get between a man and his T-bone when there are cross-hatch grill marks to be made.

But I digress. Where was I? Oh yeah, I'm pretty sure it was a woman who invented BBQ. Back in the less enlightened caveman days, the girls stayed home and kept the cave clean while the boys went out to drag back something to eat. And things were tough, let me tell you. No easy job bringing down a woolly mammoth. Yes sir, back then life pretty much revolved around what's for dinner. Except for occasionally making baby cavemen, all they ever really thought about was sleep and the next meal. And caveman cuisine was no fine dining: assorted chunks of rotting raw meat with a side of bugs, grubs and leaves. Mmmm . . . yummy. That is until someone figured out that crispy, burnt, saber-toothed bunny was way better than rabbit tartar. And that someone was most likely a woman. How else do you explain women being stuck with most of the cooking ever since?

Now granted, it was pretty hard to tell the boys from the girls back then, but it was probably a woman (ever practical) who brought that first burning stick, set afire by a bold strike of lightning, back to a cave for warmth and eventually for cooking. And by cooking we mean the charring of meat over an open flame, perfuming said meat with the subtle smoke from burning wood chips. Behold: BBQ.

Let us agree then that, regardless of gender accreditation, BBQ is the oldest form of cooking in the history of mankind. You see, there is a commonly accepted theory among many learned paleontologists that the invention of cooking (read: BBQ) was *the* seminal event that triggered an unprecedented growth in our ancestors' brain size, from the puny pound-and-a-half melon of *Homo habilis* to the three-pound monster brain of *Homo sapiens*. Therefore, it follows that the evolution of mankind and all subsequent milestones, inventions and development is because of BBQ. Yup, everything you cherish and hold dear, be it democracy, toothpaste, disco or existentialism, everything we know and everything we are is because of BBQ. Wow. That's it. That's the ultimate BBQ statement: *I BBQ, therefore I am.*

So be proud, grill jockey. Your love of cooking outdoors over open flame is embedded in your genetic code. It's like BBQ is part of your DNA. And the next time the missus wants to grill the steaks, remember – there wouldn't even be a BBQ if it wasn't for her. Step aside dude.

Which brings us to *Road Grill*, the ultimate expression of BBQ evolution. *Road Grill* is a monster. It's a huge travelling road show bringing love and BBQ to people everywhere. It takes a crew of about 40 to make an episode happen, and every episode is in a new location. Production assistants arrive on site long before the sun rises to begin building the ginormous set that features five barbecues and two prep areas wrapped in bright yellow guard rails. *Road Grill* is shot in front of a very hungry live audience in the course of one very long day that ends for those same production assistants long after the sun has gone down.

The show is hosted by Matt Dunigan, former pro quarterback, two-time Grey Cup champion, elite athlete, BBQ fanatic, and one of the nicest guys you'll ever meet. Matt grew up in the Southern United States where they take their BBQ very seriously. Matt got a hold of us when he heard we were looking for a host for a new BBQ series and, after a couple of on-camera tryouts, everyone knew he was the guy for the job. Matt has this wonderful ability to work with an audience of strangers and make them feel relaxed in the middle of all the mayhem, all the while cooking and chopping and grilling.

Matt is assisted on camera in all things BBQ by his team, namely Karrie Galvin, Charlotte Langley, and Jenna Durling. Given the size of some of our audiences, it's impossible for Matt to barbecue enough food for everyone (because they all get to eat) and host the show at the same time. Karrie, Charlotte and Jenna not only cook up a storm, they also keep Mr. Dunigan in line. The back and forth banter between them all is one of the many fun things about the show.

All the recipes in this book (and the show) were developed by Karrie Galvin and me, with Karrie doing most of the work. She and I have worked together on numerous shows and it was time for her to step into the light and have some of the fun. She is wonderful and creative and has a work ethic that would stun a team of Clydesdales.

Jenna and Charlotte are new to the television game. When I told them the hours would be stupid long, the work exhausting, and the pressure crushing, they of course didn't believe me, having both worked in fine dining kitchens. Not only did they get through it, they did so while making a huge contribution to the show. Jenna and Charlotte are both exceptional chefs and we are lucky to have them.

Kathy Doherty is Senior Producer and my de facto little sister (though much louder and more opinionated). I couldn't make television without her. Vanessa Poirier-Ogg is not only our Post Production Manager, she also did the food photography you see in this book.

This is my sixth cookbook and my fourth with McArthur & Company. I want to thank everyone over there for putting up with me and putting together yet another amazing book (you really should go out and buy the other three). Special manly shoulder punch to Kim McArthur, Taryn Manias, and Jessica Scott.

Finally, none of this would have been possible if not for Food Network Canada. Kathy Cross, Leslie Merklinger and Emily Morgan are the people there who have helped shape the show and have made *Road Grill* the juggernaut it is.

Okay, there you go. That's it. From here on in it's all BBQ all the time. Enjoy.

Chris Knight

FAQ on the BBQ

After years of shooting BBQ shows and writing BBQ books I have come to the conclusion that one must approach BBQ decisions much the way one would matters of love; always lead with your heart and everything else will follow. For BBQ must be consummated with passion and abandon, or not at all. (Except on those nights when the kids have to get to soccer and/or gymnastics and you have a migraine and the boss is on your case and there's a weird smell coming from the dog. Then it's okay to just grill the friggin' burgers and be done with it.)

Here are some of the frequently asked questions on BBQ:

What's Better, Charcoal or Gas?

Charcoal is better on paper but go with gas. Look, you can definitely achieve a higher temperature with charcoal than with most gas barbecues. You'll also spend way more time getting the charcoal lit and ready. Then there's the clean up. Gas is instantaneous and you can achieve char-inducing temperatures in a fraction of the time. Gas works just fine on 99.99% of the recipes you'll ever run across. All the recipes in this book are written for gas barbecues. If you insist on barbecuing only with charcoal then you either have way too much time on your hands or you should be doing this for a living.

How big should my BBQ be?

As with most things, size does matter. Get the biggest barbecue you can. Get a barbecue the size of a small car. Irrefutable scientific evidence clearly shows that people who own giant barbecues live longer, have nicer complexions, rarely get parking tickets and are eleven times more likely to win the lottery. At the very least, you want a barbecue that has three burners, giving you more control over temperature and more options when considering indirect barbecuing or the use of a rotisserie.

You want enough surface space on your grill to accommodate multiple burgers or chicken breasts without crowding. Crowding is bad. Crowding hinders charring and charring is good.

Also, you want a barbecue with an upper rack, known as a warming rack. This is very handy: move cooked food to the rack while you continue to barbecue other things. On the other hand, you probably already own a barbecue if you're reading this book so whatever it is you have in your backyard is perfect.

How hot should my BBQ be?

Assuming you're going with gas, you want a barbecue that pumps out around 120 BTUs per square inch of grill surface. A BTU is a British Thermal Unit, and 120 of them will get your BBQ to 550C in under 10 minutes if you crank the knobs wide open. Also, make sure the thermometer on the lid (walk away from one that doesn't have a thermometer) goes up to at least 550–600F (280–315C).

But remember that BBQ isn't just about high heat. There's all that low-heat indirect barbecuing you're going to do with ribs and butts and the like. So you want to make sure your barbecue has sensitive enough control knobs to get your heat down to around 200–225F (64–107C), otherwise you'll miss out on half the BBQ experience.

Oh and by the way, lava rocks are Old School. Get yourself a barbecue with metal "spit plates" instead. They're better heat conductors and don't require any clean up or replacement.

What tools do I need to become a BBQ master?

Excellent question. For some reason barbecue manufacturers insist on selling large and largely useless BBQ tools with wood paneling on the side. We're talking tongs that don't grip and brushes that melt and spatulas that are too short. My advice is to go to a restaurant supply store and buy your BBQ tools there. They might not be as pretty but they get the job done – and you'll look like a pro. Here's what you need:

A GOOD CLEANING BRUSH The best way to clean your grill is to crank the heat way up so that it turns any little bit of what you barbecued the last time to ashes. But the ashes cling to the grill so you need a really good brush with a really long handle (so you don't singe your knuckle hair) and brass bristles that won't melt on you.

LONG TONGS Make sure they're long enough to reach the back of your grill surface without your hand hovering over the intense heat of your mighty BBQ for any extended period of time. Also make sure they snap, as in actually have enough bite to close down on whatever you intend on tonging (hmmm…think I just invented a verb).

TWO SPATULAS – ONE LONG AND ONE OFF-SET You need a long one so you can flip a whole bunch of burgers or veggies at once. You need an offset (a bent blade) spatula to turn delicate items like certain fish fillets or crab cakes.

THERMOMETER When you've got a large cut of meat like a whole chicken or a leg of lamb you want to make sure it's cooked all the way through, so you need a good quality barbecue thermometer. I could tell you all the internal temperatures for perfectly cooked meat, but a good thermometer will have them indicated for you.

MISTER Get yourself a couple of spray bottles. Use one to douse flare ups. Use the other to spray oil on the grill.

What are the 4 most important things to remember when BBQing?

If you get nothing else from this book, remember these four rules of BBQ:

READ THE RECIPE TWICE – FROM BEGINNING TO END I cannot tell you how often someone has gotten a third of the way through preparing a meal from a cookbook, with a hungry family waiting to be fed, when they get to the instruction "and marinate for at least 12 hours." Read the recipe from beginning to end. Plus, chances are you're going to be doing something else at the same time (making a salad or grilling something else or washing the dog). By reading the recipe the second time, you get to visualize yourself doing the steps in the recipe. This is how a professional athlete gets ready – they visualize. See yourself chopping in the kitchen, then at the grill, then ducking out to pick up the kids or a bottle of wine (or both), then sitting down to dinner. Does it all make sense? Can you do it? Read the recipe twice and you'll never be flustered.

OIL THE GRILL You're going to read this in every recipe. Oil the grill (after you've cleaned it) so stuff doesn't stick. Oil the grill so you get nice char marks. This is the one thing you absolutely positively have to do every time, no exceptions.

WHEN YOU'RE GRILLIN' YOU GOTTA BE CHILLIN' This seems to be a bigger problem with the guys. Gentlemen, once you have laid that which you are grilling down on the barbecue, leave it alone. Resist the urge to stand there with your tongs and move stuff around for the sake of moving it around. Let the barbecue do the work. The only time you need to touch your food is when you're flipping it or if there's a flare up. Otherwise, go get yourself a beverage and chill.

BUY STOCK IN AN ALUMINUM FOIL COMPANY Always always always tent barbecued meat (beef, pork, poultry, lamb, veal, game, etc.) with foil and let it sit for a bit. When your steak hits the grill it tightens up in the process of cooking as the connective tissue shrinks. Juices get drawn into the middle. When you let the meat sit for a bit after coming off the grill, you let it relax and the juices flow back through the entire cut. Seriously. By tenting it with foil, you keep the heat in so it's still warm when you cut into it. How long you let it sit depends on the size of dinner. A steak needs 5 or 6 minutes. A whole leg of lamb needs about a half an hour.

What's the difference between direct and indirect BBQing?

There are both direct and indirect cooking recipes in this book. As a rule, you use direct heat when grilling over high heat for a relatively short time with the lid up. Indirect barbecuing means low heat coming from one or two burners not directly underneath your dinner for a longer period of time with the lid down. For instance, you would grill a nice rib steak directly over high heat for 5 minutes a side. You would slow smoke a brisket for a few hours with the heat on one side and the brisket on the other and the lid down to contain the smoke and regulate the temperature.

Is there any food that is not appropriate to BBQ?

Tofu, Jell-o, ice cream and Cheez Whiz. Pretty much everything else works. Okay, technically you can grill tofu but it has no business being anywhere near a BBQ.

BEEF

Beef, Veal and the Lonely Buffalo

Does anything say BBQ quite like a nice slab of red
meat sizzling on the grill? Ah beef, we have a love-hate
relationship with it. Lots of people will tell you to cut back,
that it's not good for you. Sure, one small problem though –
you're a carnivore. You are genetically predisposed
to occasionally crave a big juicy steak.
Mmmmm . . . getting hungry already!

Here is the single most important thing you need to know to BBQ beef: Find a good butcher. That's it. Take the time to find a person who specializes in selling meat. Your average mega-superstore is fine for the purchase of hygiene products and canned goods, but meat for your BBQ? C'mon. A good butcher will be your best BBQ buddy, your confidant, your guide, your BBQ guardian angel. A good butcher takes pride in his meat and will spend time with you explaining different cuts and cooking considerations. A good butcher is worth the extra five minute drive.

Buying Beef: There's only one thing you need to know when buying beef – marbling. Marbling is how the fat content looks on a piece of meat before cooking (kinda like marble). The more marbled, the more fat content. This is good. Fat is flavour, fat is your friend. You want nice marbling in your beef so that it will melt on the grill and insinuate itself through the meat leaving you a rich, beef taste. Beef is divided by "cuts" of varying quality and marbling. The only two cuts you care about are Prime and Choice. For some odd reason, Prime cuts tend to be sold only to restaurants (that's why steak tastes so much better when you eat out), so Choice is the best cut most of us can buy. Forget about cuts like Select unless you're doing a marinade and long, slow cook.

Your basic cow is divided into eight areas called primal cuts which the butcher then chops into secondary cuts that are in turn sold to me and you. But you don't need to know that. What you do need to know are the secondary cuts of meat that you see displayed in the butcher shop:

HANGER, SKIRT & FLANK STEAK A bit tough and definitely needs a marinade to soften it up. The good news is these cuts pack a deep, rich beefy flavour. Excellent grilled and sliced medium rare on sandwiches or as fajitas.

SIRLOIN Probably the most popular steak house order. Nice marbling and firm texture so it holds up well on the grill. There are sub-cuts to Sirloin, but Top Sirloin is by far the best.

TENDERLOIN This is the cut-with-a-butter-knife cut. It's incredibly tender and soft. It does not, however, have much (if any) marbling, so the taste is very mild. The FILET MIGNON is a sub-cut of Tenderloin

STRIP STEAK Very tender with a good amount of marbling. It's a nice change if you're a Sirloin lover.

T-BONE So called because it has a big bone running through it that sort of looks like a wonky "T." Look at your T-bone. The smaller cut on the left of the bone is tenderloin, while the bigger slice on the right is strip steak. Hey, two steaks for the price of one. Plus you get to cook on the bone which is always a good thing. A PORTERHOUSE STEAK is simply a very thick T-bone.

RIB STEAK My personal favourite as it is medium tender with lots of marbling and nice big rib bone attached. Always cook bone-on whenever you can as it adds beaucoup flavour.

RIB-EYE Think rib steak without the rib. It's a great steak but why would you forego that nice bone?

FLATIRON Not as popular a cut because it has a ribbon of gristle running through it. Less expensive and very tasty. Ask your butcher for a Flatiron and see how impressed he is.

TRI-TIP This is what's called a Bottom Sirloin roast and kind of looks like a triangle. It is very lean and tender and best used cut into chunks for kabobs.

RIB ROAST Think of a whole bunch of rib steaks stuck together. Mmmm. This one costs a mortgage payment but so worth it on special occasions.

BRISKET This is a tough cut so it's quite inexpensive. It's perfect for your secret marinade and a long, slow smoking on a lazy Saturday afternoon. Plus it can feed an entire softball team.

SHORT RIBS Ribs that are, well, short and from the front of the cow (called the chuck). Great for smoking or grilling after a nice marinade or rub.

BEEF RIBS Not to be confused with short ribs. These are the same ribs you'd find flavouring a rib roast. They're long and meaty and they used to be quite inexpensive till chi-chi chefs re-discovered them and made them all the rage.

Before and After: The last 2 things you need to know before slapping that steak on the BBQ is the Before and After. Always bring your meat to room temperature before barbecuing to ensure even cooking. And remember: always tent your meat with tin foil after barbecuing to allow the meat to "relax" and the juices to resettle throughout the cut.

And now a word about veal: Veal, for those of you who don't know, is baby cow, dispatched before muscles can develop, oxygenate and turn red. Some people have a problem with the consumption of veal because, in many cases, it is milk fed and kept in stalls. Fair enough. Here's one more reason to get yourself an excellent butcher who sells "natural veal" and by this we mean calves that have been allowed to graze instead of being penned up. Besides, natural veal has a more pronounced flavour and better texture.

As for the lonely buffalo, check out the third recipe in this chapter.

ALBERTA BEEF DIP SANDWICH

This beef dip sandwich is perfect with the sweet potato fries (on page 182).
I like some hot mustard spread on my bun and a big crack of fresh pepper
and some pickled veggies. You can serve the beef slices at room temperature
with a warmed up dip sauce. Serves: 10

1 6-lb (2.7 kg) sirloin tip roast with good
 marbling of fat

Marinade:

1/2 cup (125 ml) olive oil

2 teaspoons (10 ml) finely chopped garlic

1 tablespoon (15 ml) fresh rosemary,
 roughly chopped

1 tablespoon (15 ml) fresh oregano, minced

1/2 cup (125 ml) dark beer

Salt and pepper to taste

10 large crusty hoagie buns

Dipping sauce:

2 cups (500 ml) low-sodium beef stock

1 cup (250 ml) dark beer

2 sprigs fresh rosemary

1 large Spanish onion, sliced thin

Salt and pepper

- In a medium bowl combine all marinade
  ingredients (excluding the salt and pepper).

- Place the roast in a large sealable baggie and pour
  the marinade over. Marinate roast in the
  refrigerator for 4–6 hours.

- Preheat barbecue to 325F (160C) leaving the
  middle burner off.

- Remove roast from marinade and discard excess.
  Season with salt and pepper.

- Mount roast on rotisserie following manufacturer's
  instructions, and place a drip pan over the grate
  without heat.

- Pour all the dipping sauce ingredients into the drip
  pan.

- Close barbecue lid and cook for 2 1/2–3 hours,
  basting occasionally with the drippings from the
  drip pan.

- Check the roast by inserting an instant read
  thermometer in the centre of the roast. For medium
  rare: 125F (51C).

- Remove roast, cover loosely with foil and rest for
  20 minutes.

- Remove the drip pan using barbecue gloves. Strain
  the liquid using a fine mesh strainer into a small
  saucepan and simmer over low heat for 5 minutes.
  Skim any excess fat or impurities in the liquid.

- Slice beef thinly across the grain. Serve on crusty
  bread with a small bowl of warm jus for dipping.

BEEF & LAMB BASEBALL "SLIDERS"

I suppose we could get our collective butts sued for using the term "slider" since the White Castle restaurant chain holds a US trademark on the word "slyder," referring to a large number of small hamburgers. White Castle came up with the multi mini-burger concept as hamburger sales tanked post-WW2. In fact, hamburgers were commonly referred as "Salisbury steak" during this time because of the general negative sentiment toward everything German. Sort of like "freedom fries." Whatever you call them, these little guys are dee-licious. Ancho chili powder is my favourite go-to spice these days bringing both heat and a unique flavour. If you can't find mini burger buns then those little pita pockets work too. Yield: 24 mini burgers

Lamb:

2 lb (900 g) ground lamb

Zest of two lemons

1 teaspoon (5 ml) ground cumin

1 tablespoon (15 ml) roughly chopped
  oil-soaked sun-dried tomatoes

2 tablespoons (30 ml) chopped parsley,
  stems removed

2 teaspoons (10 ml) minced garlic

1 cup (250 ml) goat cheese, crumbled

Pepper to taste

12 mini hamburger buns

Olive oil for brushing

Olive tapanade and fresh arugula leaves
  for garnish (optional)

For the lamb burgers:

- Mix together the ground lamb, lemon zest, cumin, parsley, chopped sun-dried tomatoes and garlic.

- Make 24 1/4-inch patties. Try to make the rounds all equal in diameter and thickness.

- Divide the cheese into 12 portions and press into the centre of 12 patties. Top each patty with a non-cheese-filled round of beef. Seal the 2 patties together using your fingertips. Drizzle oil on both sides and season with salt and pepper.

- Preheat barbecue to medium high: 375F (190C). Oil the grill.

- Place burgers on direct heat and cook for 3–4 minutes per side or until desired doneness.

- Remove from grill, and serve each with your selected garnishes.

(Note: No salt for the lamb burgers, as the sun-dried tomatoes can be slightly salty)

Beef:

2 lb (900 g) ground medium beef

1 teaspoon (5 ml) Ancho chili powder

Salt and pepper to taste

1/2 cup (125 ml) Gorgonzola cheese

12 mini hamburger buns

Red onion and sprouts for garnish (optional)

Olive oil for brushing

For the beef burgers:

- In a medium bowl combine Ancho powder, pepper and beef, mix just to combine.

- Repeat the above procedure for making the patties but substitute with the Gorgonzola cheese.

BUFFALO BURGERS WITH OKA CHEESE

Okay, buffalo isn't beef. But we're not going to do a whole new chapter for one recipe so we put it in with beef. Buffalo is way leaner than your regular grocery store red meat and its taste is more pronounced but that is not to say it's what is euphemistically called "gamey." We've become so used to our mass-produced meat tasting like nothing that when we bite into something like buffalo or lamb we decide it's gamey. It's not – it's flavourful.

Yield: 6

2 1/4 lb (1.02 kg) ground buffalo meat

1/4 cup (60 ml) diced red onion

1/4 cup (60 ml) sun-dried cranberries, chopped

1 teaspoon (5 ml) fresh ground pepper

Salt to taste

Olive oil for brushing

6 slices Oka cheese

6 hamburger buns

1 cup (250 ml) store-bought apple cranberry chutney

Optional garnish: mayonnaise, red onion slices, lettuce

- In a medium bowl mix together ground meat, onion, cranberries, salt and pepper until well combined.

- Form into 6 equal patties being careful not to overwork the meat. Brush each side lightly with olive oil.

- Preheat grill to medium high: 375F (190C). Oil the grill.

- Place burgers on grill and cook 3–4 minutes per side for medium rare. Buffalo is lean meat and doesn't take well to overcooking. These burgers should be served medium rare.

- Flip and in the last minute of cooking top burgers with cheese, close the barbecue lid.

- Remove from grill when cheese has melted.

- Serve with red onion, lettuce, mayonnaise and cranberry chutney if desired.

FLANK STEAK FAJITA

Fajita is the Spanish word for "grossly overpriced lunch or dinner item served in a Big Box restaurant at the end of a Big Box parking lot." Or not. It takes about the same time for you to barbecue dinner as it does for you to drive to some chain restaurant where the primary seasoning is salt. But you already know that. That's why you bought this book. That's why you own a BBQ. That's why you're going to heaven. Serves 4–6

1 whole flank steak

2 limes, zested and juiced

1/4 cup (60 ml) vegetable oil

6–8 soft tortilla shells

Oil for brushing

Salt and pepper to taste

Rub:

1 tablespoon (15 ml) chili powder

1 teaspoon (5 ml) ground coriander

1 1/2 teaspoons (7.5 ml) ground cumin

1/2 teaspoon (2.5 ml) garlic powder

1/2 teaspoon (2.5 ml) black pepper

Summer salsa:

3–4 large ripe tomatoes, finely diced

2–3 green onions, sliced thin

1 yellow bell pepper, seeded, diced

1 red bell pepper, seeded, diced

1/2 cup (125 ml) finely chopped red onion

3 tablespoons (45 ml) chopped cilantro leaves

Juice of 1 lime or 2 depending on how juicy

1/2 jalapeno pepper, seeded, finely diced

Salt and pepper to taste

Optional garnishes: sour cream, cilantro, peppers, and guacamole.

- Place steak in a non-reactive container.

- Combine all rub spices in a small bowl mix until evenly combined. Rub all over steak with slight pressure to tear little micro pockets of flavour into the meat.

- Zest the limes and squeeze juice over steak. Drizzle steak with oil.

- Marinate overnight in the refrigerator.

- Remove steak from refrigerator 30 minutes before cooking and season with salt and pepper and drizzle with oil.

- Preheat barbecue to high: 475F–500F (246C–260C). Oil grill.

- Place steak directly on grill and cook for 3 minutes or until nice golden char marks are achieved. Give the steak a quarter turn and grill a further 2 minutes. Flip and repeat.

- Remove from grill, cover loosely with foil and let rest 15 minutes.

- In a medium bowl combine all salsa ingredients. Season to taste with salt and pepper.

- Just before you are ready to serve, preheat barbecue to medium: 350F (176C). Place tacos in foil and warm on the barbecue for 2 minutes with lid down.

- Cut the meat against the grain in thin slices and serve with fresh salsa and warm taco shells.

CHIPOTLE VEAL CHOPS WITH FUJI APPLE CHUTNEY

Remember to cook bone-on whenever possible as it adds flavour to the meat. Chipotles are smoked jalapeno peppers smothered in a spicy tomato sauce called adobo sauce. Use Granny Smith if you can't find Fuji apples. The chutney works nicely with the heat from the chipotle marinade. Yield: 6 Servings

6 bone-in veal chops, each 1 inch (15 cm) thick

2 tablespoons (30 ml) fresh chopped cilantro

2 whole chipotle chilies in adobo sauce,
   minced fine

1/2 cup (125 ml) olive oil

Fuji apple chutney:

2 cups (500 ml) Fuji apples peeled, cored
   and cut into 1/4 inch dice

2 tablespoons (30 ml) fresh lemon juice

1 tablespoon (15 ml) vegetable oil

3/4 cup (190 ml) Spanish onions, finely diced

1 tablespoon (15 ml) finely minced ginger

1/2 cup (125 ml) rice wine vinegar

1/2 cup (125 ml) unsweetened apple juice

Salt and pepper to taste

- In a medium bowl combine the chopped chipotle, oil and cilantro. Place veal in a large sealable bag and pour the marinade over to coat the veal evenly.

- Refrigerate for 4 hours.

Apple chutney:

- In a large, non-reactive bowl, toss the apples with the lemon juice.

- Heat oil in a large saucepan at medium-high for 30 seconds. Add the onions and ginger and sauté until onions are translucent and fragrant, 3–4 minutes.

- Add the apples and cook for 3–4 minutes. Add the vinegar and apple juice and cook until liquid is reduced by half.

- Season with salt and pepper to taste and cool to room temperature.

- Preheat barbecue to medium high: 375F (190C). Oil grill.

- Remove veal from marinade and season with salt and pepper. Grill for 3–4 minutes per side or until nice char marks are achieved.

- Remove from grill and serve hot with the Fuji apple chutney.

GRILLED RIB STEAK
WITH CHIPOTLE BUTTER

Pound for pound I think the rib steak is the best combination of flavour and texture of all the cuts out there. Always remember to bring a steak to room temperature before BBQing and to tent it after it comes off the grill. Chipotle butter gives the steak a big whack of heat and smoky flavour. Yield: 6 Servings

6 rib steaks, 10 oz (284 g) each

Salt and pepper

Olive oil for brushing

Butter:

1/2 cup (125 ml) unsalted butter

1 whole chipotle chili in adobo sauce,
  minced fine

2 tablespoons (30 ml) cilantro leaves
  finely chopped

2 tablespoons (30 ml) fine chopped red onion

For butter:

- Combine butter ingredients in a food processor and process until completely mixed.

- Spread butter onto a piece of plastic wrap or parchment paper and roll up the butter to make a log 1 inch (15 cm) in diameter. Refrigerate at least 30 minutes.

For the steak:

- Preheat barbecue to high heat: 500–600F (260–315C). Oil grill.

- Allow steaks to come to room temperature. Drizzle with the olive oil and season with salt and pepper.

- Place steak directly on the hot grill. Cook for 3 minutes or until a dark caramelized crust is achieved. Give the steak a quarter turn and grill a further 3 minutes for medium rare. Flip steak and cook for 4–5 minutes longer.

- Remove from grill onto a platter and top with a 1/2 inch slice of the butter. Cover the plate loosely with foil and rest meat for 10 minutes.

HERBED SMOKED PRIME RIB OF BEEF WITH GARLIC AND HORSERADISH

Okay, so this recipe calls for "prepared horseradish." Prepared means the stuff you get in a jar, all diced up and almost creamy. It's okay as prepared foods go but it is so much better if you can get your hands on the real fresh root. It really doesn't have much of a scent until you peel it and then wham – pungent, clean horseradish clears the cobwebs. If the herbs listed below are not available then substitute whatever you can get that's fresh. The whole idea is to perfume the outer crust of your roast so your dinner guests' eyes roll back in their heads with delight. Serve with the barbecued Yorkshire pudding on page 154. Serves 8–10

4–5 lb (1.81–2.26 kg) bone-in prime rib
    of beef with a good fat cap

Wet rub:
1 tablespoon (15 ml) garlic minced
1 tablespoon (15 ml) prepared horseradish
1/2 cup (125 ml) mixed fresh herbs such as
    rosemary, savory, oregano and thyme
3 tablespoons (45 ml) olive oil
Salt and freshly ground pepper to taste

Smoke pouch:
8 bundles of dried herbs such as thyme,
    savory and rosemary.
Place half of the herbs in cool water
    for 30 minutes.

- Combine all ingredients for the wet rub in a small bowl. Rub all over the beef to evenly coat and place on a large roasting pan.

- Prepare 2 smoke pouches by placing equal parts dry and wet herbs onto 2 large squares of foil. Wrap the foil packages into a size slightly smaller than your barbecue burner. Using the tines of a fork, poke all over to allow smoke to escape.

- Prepare barbecue for indirect smoking by placing 2 burners on high and removing grates. Leave one side of the barbecue off.

- Preheat barbecue to 325F–335F. (160C–170C). Place the smoke pouch on the burner with heat; close lid and wait for smoke.

- Place the beef in the roasting pan on the indirect side and close lid. Baste every 1/2 hour with the pan drippings and change the herb smoke pouch when the smoke dissipates.

- Allow to slow roast for 15–20 minutes per pound, depending on how you like your beef. Or better yet, check the temperature by inserting a thermometer in the centre of the roast away from the bone.

- Once cooked to your desired temperature, remove from barbecue, loosely cover with foil and let the meat rest for 20 minutes before carving.

- Serve with horseradish sauce.

Don't throw away the pan drippings! Use them to make classic Yorkshire pudding. Learn how on page 154.

HUNAN SLOW-SMOKED BEEF RIBS

"Hunan" is a province in China and "hoisin" is a soy-based salty, thick,
delicious sauce (think Asian ketchup). Make this one time and you'll be
making it for the rest of your life. As with any BBQ recipe, it is your destiny
as a BBQ-ologist to adjust the ingredients below to create your own unique
rib dish. I know it looks like a whole bunch of work but please read the
recipe. It's not as hard as it seems. Ribs never are. Yield: 2 full racks of ribs

2 whole racks of beef ribs, 8 bones each rack

Rub:

4 teaspoons (20 ml) Chinese five-spice powder

2 tablespoons (30 ml) salt

*1 tablespoon (15 ml) freshly ground black
    pepper*

*2 tablespoons (30 ml) lightly packed
    brown sugar*

2 teaspoons (10 ml) chili flakes

Sauce:

2 cups (500 ml) hoisin sauce

Juice of 3 oranges

2 tablespoons (30 ml) grated ginger

1 1/2 tablespoons (22.5 ml) chopped garlic

1/4 cup (60 ml) dry sherry

2 tablespoons (30 ml) sesame seeds

*9 cups (2.25 kg) apple wood chips. Soak 6
cups (1.5 L) of the wood chips in cool water
    for 1 hour and drain.*

- In a small bowl combine all rub ingredients and stir to combine evenly. Rub all over the ribs using slight pressure to tear the micro fibres of the meat.

- Place in a large baggie and refrigerate overnight.

- Combine all the hoisin sauce ingredients in a medium bowl.

- Make 3 smoke pouches. Learn how on page 37.

- Prepare barbecue for indirect smoking by leaving 2 burners off and one burner on high with the grate removed. Preheat to 220F (104C).

- Place a smoke pouch over the high heat side and place a drip pan under the grates without heat.

- Place the ribs over the drip pan, close lid and smoke for 2 1/2 hours. Change the smoke pouch when smoke dissipates.

- After 2 1/2 hours, baste ribs with the hoisin sauce. Close lid and continue to cook for 1 hour, basting every 30 minutes. Ribs will be done when you can pull them easily from the bone.

- Remove ribs from grill, loosely tent with foil and let rest for 20 minutes.

- Using a sharp knife, slice ribs between bones and serve with leftover sauce.

KICK-ASS SIRLOIN STEAK SANDWICHES

By "kick-ass" we mean amazing, supreme, the best, incomparable. It's just more fun to say kick-ass. This is a high-end version of the Philly steak sandwich minus the cheese. Another way to do it is to substitute well-marinated hanger or flank steak. Just *puh-lease* don't overcook.

Yield: 6–8 big-ass sandwiches

1 2-inch thick whole sirloin steak with
   good marbling

2 teaspoons (10 ml) cracked black pepper

2 teaspoon (10 ml) mixed Italian dried herbs

Salt to taste

2 tablespoons (30 ml) olive oil

1 red bell pepper cut into 1/4-inch strips
   lengthwise

1 yellow bell pepper cut into 1/4-inch
   strips lengthwise

1 small onion sliced thin

1 tablespoon (15 ml) garlic oil

Salt and pepper to taste

Garlic bread:

1 large loaf of Italian bread

1 tablespoon (15 ml) fresh minced garlic

1/4 cup (60 ml) butter softened

2 tablespoons (30 ml) fresh chopped parsley

2 cups (500 ml) mixed spring lettuce

For the bread:

- In a medium bowl mix together the butter, garlic, parsley, salt and pepper. Slice the baguette lengthwise and spread butter mixture all over bread.

- Wrap bread in foil and heat for 4 minutes on the barbecue warming rack when you are ready to grill the steak.

For the peppers and onions:

- Place the peppers and onions in a bowl. Drizzle with garlic oil, salt and pepper.

- Preheat barbecue to high: 475F–500F (246C–260C).

- Preheat a grill basket for 10 minutes. Place the vegetables directly into the basket. Cook, stirring occasionally until nice golden char marks are achieved. Remove from grill.

For the steak:

- Rub steak all over with olive oil, pepper, herbs and salt.

- Preheat barbecue to high: 475F–500F (246C–260C). Oil grill.

- Place steak on grill and cook until nice char marks are achieved – about 5–6 minutes. Give the steak a quarter turn and continue cooking until a full diamond char mark is achieved, about 4 minutes. Flip and repeat process.

- Remove from grill, cover with foil and allow the meat to rest 10–12 minutes.

- Slice steak and pile on top of warmed bread, add the peppers and lettuce. Close baguette and cut loaf into 2-inch pieces.

ROASTED 3 PEPPERCORN BEEF TENDERLOIN WITH CHERRY SAUCE

Happily, fresh cherries coincide with the beginning of BBQ season in many parts of North America. So celebrate by buying yourself some new rubber gloves to wear when you pit the cherries, otherwise you'll end up with blood-red hands. As this is a reduction, inexpensive grocery store balsamic will do instead of the more pricey stuff you drizzle on a salad. Serves 4

1 whole beef tenderloin, silver skin removed

2 teaspoons (10 ml) pink peppercorns

2 teaspoons (10 ml) whole Szechwan
  peppercorns

1 teaspoon (5 ml) whole black peppercorns

1 tablespoon (15 ml) fresh roughly
  chopped rosemary

2 tablespoons (30 ml) olive oil

2 teaspoons (10 ml) kosher salt

Cherry Sauce:

2 cups (500 ml) red wine, like a rich Cabernet

1 whole shallot, diced fine

1 sprig fresh rosemary

1 tablespoon (15 ml) fresh sliced ginger

1 tablespoon (15 ml) balsamic vinegar

2 cups (500 ml) fresh pitted cherries

Salt to taste

- To make the sauce, combine the wine, shallot, ginger and rosemary in a medium saucepan over medium heat and bring to a gentle boil.

- Reduce heat to low and simmer until reduced by half. Strain the liquid using a fine mesh strainer. Add the sliced cherries and balsamic vinegar while wine mixture is still hot. Season with salt.

- Place peppercorns in a coffee grinder and use pulse feature until the peppercorns are broken and smashed. Place the cracked peppercorns in a bowl; stir in the rosemary and salt, then rub the peppercorn mixture all over beef.

- Place beef on a tray and let it come to room temperature. This will help the beef cook evenly for a perfect medium rare. Brush with oil and sprinkle with salt.

- Preheat your barbecue for medium-high: 375F-425F (190C-218C). Leave one burner off. Oil grill.

- Place the tenderloin on the hot side of the grill and cook with lid open until nice char marks are achieved, about 3–4 minutes per side. Turn the beef, continuing to char the entire outside.

- Once lovely char marks are achieved move beef over to the indirect side (no heat) of the barbecue. Close the lid and continue to cook for 20–25 minutes or until desired doneness.

- The best way to determine doneness is by inserting a thermometer in the thickest part of the tenderloin.

- Remove beef from grill, tent with foil and let rest for 15–20 minutes. Slice the beef and serve with the cherry sauce.

KOREAN GRILLED BEEF SATAY WITH SOY GINGER DIPPING SAUCE

Please note that I like to use about three times the amount of garlic we call for in this recipe. This of course is a fundamental precept of the BBQ mindset. To wit: adapt and reinvent all recipes to suit your own personal tastes. We use lettuce leaves to wrap the lean marinated pork but you could just as easily use soft tortillas if you'd like. Rather than "Tex-Mex" you'll have "Mexi-Ko" (har har). Yield: 24 kabobs

1 1/4 lb (565 g) beef tenderloin, 5 inches
   (8 cm) in length, silver skin removed

1 cup (250 ml) low-sodium soy sauce

3 large garlic cloves, minced fine

1 tablespoon (15 ml) fresh grated ginger

1 tablespoon (15 ml) sugar

3 tablespoons (45 ml) toasted sesame seeds

1 tablespoon (15 ml) sesame oil

1/4 cup (60 ml) sake wine or white wine

3 green onions, white and light green parts
   only, minced fine

3 green onions, sliced thin

24 bibb lettuce leaves

1 small seedless cucumber, peeled and
   sliced into thin matchsticks

1 carrot cut into thin matchsticks

Pepper to taste

Oil for brushing

24 8-inch (13 cm) skewers soaked in
   cool water for 30 minutes

- In a large nonreactive bowl, combine the soy sauce, garlic, ginger, sugar, pepper, sesame seeds, sesame oil, and sake. Add the finely chopped green onion and stir.

- Place 1/2 cup of the marinade in a saucepan set over medium heat, bring to a boil and cook for 30 seconds. Reserve.

- Slice the fillet into 1/4-inch thick pieces, cutting lengthwise with the grain. Then slice each piece again lengthwise into 1–1 1/2-inch (1.5–2 cm) pieces. Depending on the exact width of the meat, you should have about 24 pieces.

- Transfer meat strips to the marinade, cover and refrigerate for 1 hour and remove from marinade 20 minutes before cooking.

- Preheat barbecue to moderate high: 450F (232C). Oil grill.

- Thread the meat onto the soaked bamboo skewers. Pierce the meat about 4 times so that it stretches along the length of the skewer.

- Place meat on the grill and cook for 1 minute per side or just until the meat has deep char marks.

- Arrange lettuce leaves on a serving platter, fill each leaf with cucumber, carrot and sliced green onion.

- Serve sauce in a long shallow dish. The best way to eat these is to pick up the lettuce leaf, dip the skewered meat into the sauce, then wrap the leaf around the whole thing and slide it off the skewer.

SMOKED VEAL RIB CHOP ROAST IN A MAPLE BOURBON MARINADE

This is definitely a grown-up dinner party recipe. Sit back and drink in the applause after your guests take that first bite of tender juicy veal, flavoured with maple syrup, Dijon and whisky and kissed with a subtle suggestion of apple wood smoke. Serve this up with the Pear & Fennel Salad found on page 150. Yield: 6–8 servings

6 lb (2.72 kg) veal rib roast, bone in

1 cup (250 ml) white onion, chopped fine

1/2 cup (125 ml) fresh orange juice

2 teaspoons (5 ml) finely chopped garlic

1 tablespoon (15 ml) minced ginger

1/4 cup (60 ml) bourbon whisky

3 tablespoons (45 ml) maple syrup

2 tablespoons (30 ml) cider vinegar

2 teaspoons (10 ml) hot sauce

1/2 cup (125 ml) canola oil

Salt and pepper to taste

Oil for brushing

6 cups (1.5 L) apple wood chips.
    Soak 4 cups (1 L) of the chips in water
    for 1 hour and drain.

- Place all marinade ingredients into a large bowl and whisk to combine. Reserve 1/2 cup for basting.

- Place veal roast in a large sealable baggie. Pour the marinade over and toss to evenly coat the veal. Marinate in the refrigerator for 4–6 hours.

- Prepare barbecue for indirect smoking and cooking. Leave one burner on and the other two off. Place a drip pan under the grills that are off. Preheat the barbecue to 220F (104C).

- Prepare smoke pouches (see page 37.) Place smoke pouch directly on the gas burner over direct heat.

- Remove the veal from the marinade, drizzle with olive oil, season with salt and pepper, and place on the grill over the drip pan. Close the lid and smoke veal for 1 hour, changing the smoke pouch when smoke dissipates.

- After 1 hour start basting the veal with the reserved marinade. Continue to cook for 1 more hour or until the temperature reaches 140F (60C).

- Remove veal; loosely cover with foil and rest the meat for 15 minutes.

TRIPLE PLAY SMOKED MUSHROOM VEAL LOIN

I know, I know. You're scratching your head and saying jeez, there's a lot to do in this recipe. Listen, you can't do burgers and chicken breasts for the rest of your BBQ life. You gotta stretch and find your inner BBQ ninja. Read through the recipe. You'll see that there's not a lot of difficult stuff here. I promise, you can do it. Serves 6

1 4-lb (1.8 kg) boneless veal loin,
   silver skin removed

1 pound (454 g) mixed mushrooms
   such as oyster, king and chanterelle

2 lemons, zested and juiced

4 cloves garlic, finely chopped

3 tablespoons (45 ml) chopped tarragon

2 tablespoons (30 ml) olive oil

Salt and pepper to taste

Marinade:

1 cup (250 ml) white wine

1/4 cup (60 ml) olive oil

Zest of 2 lemons

2 sprigs fresh tarragon

1/4 cup (60 ml) white onion, chopped fine

1 teaspoon (5 ml) finely chopped garlic

Olive oil for brushing

1 cup (250 ml) white wine for the drip pan

Lemon and tarragon for garnish (optional)

6 cups (1.5 L) cherry wood chips, 4 of the
   cups (1 L) soaked in cool water for 1 hour
   and drained

- Place all ingredients for the marinade in a small bowl. Whisk until evenly combined.

- Place the veal in a large sealable plastic baggie. Pour the marinade over and marinate in the refrigerator for 4–6 hours.

- Clean mushrooms well using a mushroom brush. Drizzle with olive oil and toss with garlic, pepper and lemon zest.

Don't add salt to mushrooms before you cook them as it draws out moisture and they will steam rather sear.

- Preheat barbecue to medium high: 375F (190C). Preheat a grill basket for 10 minutes with the lid closed. Using a cloth, carefully oil the basket. Place all mushrooms in basket and cook while stirring for 7–8 minutes, or until caramelized sear marks are achieved.

- Remove from grill, sprinkle with salt, lemon juice and the fresh chopped tarragon. Cool the mushrooms and roughly chop into 1/2-inch pieces.

- Remove veal from the baggie, place on a meat cutting board and pat off excess marinade. Using a sharp knife, make an even slice through the centre of the loin, holding the blade parallel to the work surface, but do not slice through – leave about an inch uncut. Open the butterflied meat. It should be an even thickness throughout. If not, gently pound with a meat mallet for an even thickness.

- Season the inside and outside with salt and pepper. Distribute the mushroom filling equally down the centre of the roast. Tie the roast the old-fashioned way with butcher's twine – probably 8 ties – to ensure the filling will not pop out and the roast cooks evenly.

- Prepare smoke pouches (see below.) Preheat barbecue to low: 220F (104C) on one side with no heat on the other side. Place a smoke pouch directly over the heat source and slide a drip pan under the no heat side. Add the wine to the drip pan. Oil grill.

To make smoke pouches:

Place 1 part dry and 2 parts wet chips onto a large square of foil. Wrap the foil into packages slightly smaller than your BBQ burner. Using the tines of a fork, poke package all over to allow smoke to escape.

- Place veal roast over the drip pan on the no heat side. Close the lid and smoke for 20 minutes per pound or until desired doneness. Replace the smoke pouch when smoke dissipates.

- Remove veal from the barbecue, cover loosely with foil and let rest 15–20 minutes.

- Slice into 1/2-inch (1.3 cm) slices, drizzle with lemon and sprinkle the centre with salt and optional garnish before serving.

VEAL LOIN WITH PANCETTA AND LEMON CAPER SAUCE

Veal loin is very lean which means it has a subtle, delicate flavour that lends itself to the saltiness of the pancetta which in turn plays off the tartness of the lemon caper sauce. This works really well with the grilled asparagus on page 158. Serves 6–8

1 5-lb (2.26) boneless veal loin, silver skin
    removed

Marinade:

1 cup (250 ml) white onion, medium dice

1 tablespoon (15 ml) roughly chopped
    fresh sage leaves

1 teaspoon (5 ml) lemon zest

2 teaspoons (10 ml) minced garlic

1 cup (250 ml) white wine

1/4 cup (60 ml) olive oil

1 teaspoon (5 ml) freshly ground pepper

14 slices pancetta ham

Sauce:

2 tablespoons (30 ml) olive oil

3 tablespoons (45 ml) chopped white onion

2 tablespoons (30 ml) sliced green onion

2 teaspoons (10 ml) minced garlic

3 tablespoons (45 ml) capers

1/2 cup (125 ml) white wine

1/2 cup (125 ml) chicken stock

1 teaspoon (5 ml) Dijon mustard

1/4 cup (l60 ml) lemon juice

Freshly ground pepper to taste

- Combine marinade ingredients in a small bowl.

- Place the veal loin in a large sealable baggie, cover with the marinade and place in the refrigerator to marinate 4–6 hours.

- Remove veal from the marinade, pat dry and season with pepper.

- Place the pancetta slices on a piece of plastic wrap overlapping to form a rectangle the size of the roast. Place the seasoned roast at the edge of the pancetta and roll up. Ensure that the entire roast is covered with the bacon and an overlapping seam of bacon is created. Twist the ends of the plastic wrap to secure.

- Place in the refrigerator to set up for 30 minutes.

For the sauce:

- Warm the olive oil in a large skillet set over medium-high heat for 1 minute. Add the onions, garlic and capers and sauté until onions are translucent.

- Deglaze the pan with the white wine. Cook a further 2 minutes; add the chicken stock, lemon juice, Dijon and salt and pepper. Simmer for 5 minutes over moderate heat. Remove from heat, taste and adjust seasoning.

For the veal:

- Prepare barbecue for indirect heat leaving 2 burners off and one burner on. Preheat to 275F (135C). Place a drip pan under the grills with the burners off.

- Remove the plastic wrap from the veal and drizzle with oil and pepper.

- Oil the grills of the barbecue. Place the veal on hot side of the grill and cook for 1–2 minutes on each side until the bacon is dark pink in colour with slight caramelized brown char marks.

- Move veal to the indirect side of the barbecue over the drip pan. Close lid and cook the veal for about 1 1/2 hours or until desired doneness. An instant read thermometer in the centre of the roast should read 145F (62C).

- Remove the roast and let rest uncovered for 10 minutes.

- Carve into 1/2-inch thick slices using a sharp knife to ensure the pancetta is secured around each portion. Rewarm the sauce and spoon generously over veal.

Veal should never be served well done – it should be pink.

VEAL MEDALLIONS WITH NECTARINE GINGER

Veal loin is lean with a mild delicate taste so don't overcook. You can double up on the chutney recipe and keep some in the fridge for a good week. It works nicely with other grilled meats like chicken or tuna steak. Serves 6

12 veal medallions 1-inch- (15 cm-) thick,
    cut from the loin
1/4 cup olive oil
Salt and pepper to taste

Chutney:

2 tablespoons (30 ml) vegetable oil

1/2 cup (125 ml) red onion, finely chopped

2 teaspoons (10 ml) chopped garlic

2 tablespoons (30 ml) minced fresh ginger

1/2 teaspoon (2.5 ml) ground cinnamon

Dash of ground cardamom

Juice of 3 large sweet oranges

Zest of 1 orange

Juice of 1 lime

1/4 cup (60 ml) rice wine vinegar

2 tablespoons (30 ml) brown sugar

6 fresh, ripe nectarines pitted and cut
    into thin slices

1/4 cup (60 ml) fresh mint leaves, chopped

Salt and pepper to taste

- To make the chutney, warm the oil in a medium saucepan over high heat. Add the onion, garlic, ginger, cinnamon and cardamom and sauté until onion is translucent and mixture is fragrant.

- Add the orange juice and zest, lime juice, rice wine vinegar and sugar. Reduce heat to medium; cook until slightly thickened; about 5 minutes.

- Stir in half of the nectarines and cook a further 4 minutes. Remove from heat, add the remaining nectarines and fresh mint. Season with salt and pepper.

- Preheat barbecue to moderate high: 475F (245C). Oil grill.

- Brush the veal with olive oil and season with salt and pepper.

- Grill for approximately 2 minutes per side or until desired doneness. (Veal is best served when still very pink in the centre.)

- Remove from grill, place 2 medallions on each plate and top with chutney.

PORK

Homer: Pork chops and bacon, my two favorite animals . . . Are you saying you're never going to eat any animal again? What about bacon?

Lisa: No.

Homer: Ham?

Lisa: No.

Homer: Pork chops?

Lisa: Dad, those all come from the same animal.

Homer: Heh heh heh. Ooh, yeah, right, Lisa. A wonderful, magical animal.

Ah, the pig. The venerable cochon. Much like poultry, pork has long been a mystery meat. By that I mean we've been buying pork without knowing its breed or provenance. We go into the store and buy ribs or roasts without a clue where Mr. Pig came from. The Spanish love their pigs. In Spain, they know where a pig comes from and what breed it is. They know what it ate. They know how it was dispatched and when. Those Spaniards take their pig seriously because they take their sausage seriously.

I'm happy to say things are changing here in North America. More and more people are starting to pay attention to what goes down the gullet. If you're going to die (and you are) it shouldn't be from something you have control over. No, I'm *not* saying you're going to die from eating pork. But you can keel over from a crappy diet and knowing where your food comes from is one way of keeping yourself around all that much longer. There is no greater truth than "you are what you eat." Small farming co-operatives all over the place are now raising healthier breeds of pork for sale in enlightened markets (the Berkshire breed being one example). Not only is it better for you, it tastes better as well.

Homer was right. The pig is a magical animal. Save for that little tail, there is virtually no part of the pig that we do not consume in one way or another. From lowly pig's knuckles to slow-smoked sticky ribs to a proud crown roast, the pig gives it all.

For those of you out there who still think fat when you think pork, well, things have changed in the last twenty years. Pork is lean. Pork is good. Fat content (and taste) varies from cut to cut. Do not pass up the pig just because you thing he's a fatty.

A pig is divided into 4 primary cuts from which you get all the secondary cuts at your butcher. It goes something like this:

THE LOIN This is the area between the shoulder and the butt. It's the leanest and features some of the most popular store-bought cuts including baby back ribs, chops, tenderloins, and roasts.

THE BELLY Located directly underneath the loin, the belly gives up spare ribs (fattier than the back ribs from the loin) and bacon.

THE SHOULDER Up front you've got the part of the pig that's a bit tougher and fattier, giving us cuts that need a bit more love and attention. The main cuts you'll use are the Boston butt (don't ask) and shoulder roast which, when marinated, basted and slow cooked gives up juicy, tender pulled pork. You also get ham hocks from the shoulder.

THE LEG This where the ham comes from. It's that simple.

Three Questions About Pork that Keep People Up at Night:

1 WHAT MAKES FOR BETTER BBQ – BACK RIBS OR SPARE RIBS? Wars have been fought over this burning question. The answer is . . . it depends. Back ribs are leaner and require less cooking time. Some people like that. Spare ribs are fattier (and advocates insist they're therefore tastier) and require a longer cooking time. Both are delicious. Either way, make sure you (or your butcher) remove the pale skin-like membrane that covers the back of the rack. Otherwise your rack will tighten up as the membrane shrinks and becomes tough.

2 MY GRANDMA TOLD ME TO COOK PORK UNTIL IT'S GREY AND CHEWY OR I COULD DIE. WHAT'S WITH THE PINK? I'm sure your granny is a very nice person, but clearly she's not kept up with the times. Pork, like all meats sold in this country, is closely inspected before being sold to the general public. Pork is as safe as any other meat as long as you handle it properly. And, pork is so lean now that it's a bit of a challenge to cook the grilling cuts properly. Obviously, the pink debate doesn't include the slow cooked cuts like roasts and ribs. We're talking tenderloins and chops, and a rosy pink tenderloin is a beautiful, tasty thing. Think medium as opposed to medium rare. Overcooking pork is a waste. Overcooking anything is waste. Here's one more reason to invest in that handy dandy

BBQ thermometer that will tell you exactly when the centre of your loin or chop is perfect for taking off the grill.

3 SHOULD I TAKE MY PORK OFF THE GRILL AND EAT IT LIKE RIGHT AWAY THAT SECOND? OR SHOULD I COVER IT IN TIN FOIL AND LET IT REST FOR A FEW MINUTES TILL IT RELAXES AND BECOMES MORE JUICY AND DELICIOUS BECAUSE I LOVE MY FAMILY AND FRIENDS AND WOULD NOT WANT TO DENY THEM THE BEST POSSIBLE BBQ EXPERIENCE? Um, that would be no then yes. Thanks.

GARLIC AND HERB PORK CHOPS

These are not the dried up shoe-rubber pork chops you grew up with. First you get some thick centre-cut chops and then marinate them in wine and herbs and stuff till they plump up. Then you grill them . . . for no more than 5 minutes a side because you know a little pink in your pork means tender juicy meat, and leaving them on any longer will dry them out and make them inedible. And don't forget to tent them with tin foil before serving.

Yield: 6 chops

6 large, 1 1/4-inch- (3.2 cm-) thick pork
    chops, centre-cut, bone in
5 cloves garlic (2 cut in thin slices and
    3 cloves minced)
1 cup (250 ml) white wine, like a Riesling
    or Chardonnay
2 tablespoons (30 ml) olive oil
1 teaspoon (5 ml) white sugar
2 tablespoons (30 ml) fresh oregano leaves,
    roughly chopped
2 teaspoons (10 ml) fresh thyme leaves
2 tablespoons (30 ml) fresh sage, roughly
    chopped
2 tablespoons (30 ml) fresh rosemary,
    roughly chopped
Salt and pepper to taste

- Place the chops on a cutting board, using a small sharp knife, cut small slits into the sides of the chop and insert garlic slices into the slits. Place the chops in a large plastic baggie.

- In a blender, combine the wine, oil, minced garlic and sugar. Blend on high speed. Add the fresh herbs, salt and pepper and continue to blend until smooth.

- Pour the marinade over the chops and marinate in the refrigerator for 4 hours.

- Preheat barbecue to medium: 375F (190C) for direct grilling. Oil the grill.

- Remove the chops from the marinade and season with salt and pepper. Drizzle with oil to prevent any sticking to the grill.

- Place pork chops on the oiled grill and cook 4–5 minutes per side. Halfway through cooking give the chops a quarter turn to create a diamond pattern. Flip the chops and continue to cook a further 4–5 minutes or until desired doneness.

- Remove from grill, allow to rest under foil for 15 minutes.

JESTER'S CROWN ROAST WITH CONCORD GRAPE SAUCE

You know what a crown roast is – that big circular pork roast with all the rib bones sticking up like a crown. Don't back away from this one if you can't find Concord grapes. Just substitute 3 cups of white grape juice and a big tablespoonful of grape jelly. Yield: 8 portions

1 full crown roast of pork

Rub:

2 tablespoons (30 ml) olive oil

1 tablespoon (15 ml) fresh ground pepper

1 tablespoon (15 ml) lemon zest

*1 tablespoon (15 ml) fresh thyme leaves,
   stems removed*

Salt to taste

Grape sauce:

2 lb (908 g) Concord grapes stems removed

2 sprigs fresh thyme

2 teaspoons (10 ml) whole black peppercorns

2 star anise, whole

2 cinnamon sticks, 4 inches (10 cm) each

*2 cups (500 ml) unsweetened
   white grape juice*

Salt to taste

- To make the rub, mix together the thyme, lemon zest, pepper and olive oil in a small bowl. Rub all over the roast, and marinate in the refrigerator overnight.

- Combine all the sauce ingredients in a saucepan set over medium. Bring to a boil, reduce heat to low and simmer 20 minutes.

- Strain sauce into a bowl. Season with salt to taste.

- Remove roast from refrigerator and cover the exposed bones with foil so the bones don't char and burn, as that flavour will sink down into the flesh of the meat. Season outside with salt.

- Prepare barbecue for indirect heat leaving 2 burners on medium-low and one burner off. Place a drip pan under the grill with the heat off. Close the lid and preheat barbecue to 325F (162C). Oil grill.

- Place the crown roast over the drip pan on the indirect heat side. Close lid and cook for approximately 20 minutes per pound or until an instant read thermometer inserted in the thickest part of the roast reads 150F (65C).

- Remove roast, loosely tent with foil and let meat rest 20 minutes before carving.

- To carve, simply cut evenly between each bone. Serve with warmed sauce.

GRILLED PORK TENDERLOIN WITH WILD BERRY PORT

Tenderloin is the leanest cut of pork you're likely to run across, so it cooks really quickly. Resist the urge to overcook. Because it's so lean, it has a very mild flavour and benefits from a big flavour sauce like wild berry and port. The cooking process will burn the alcohol off the port leaving that rich, intense flavour combined with whatever berries you pick up in season. This is a perfect example of how BBQ can go high-end and still be simple no-muss, no-fuss cooking. Serves 6

2 whole pork tenderloins, trimmed and
    silver skin removed
2 tablespoons (30 ml) olive oil
2 tablespoons (30 ml) fresh chopped rosemary
Salt and pepper to taste

Wild berry port sauce:

1 shallot sliced thin
2 sprigs fresh thyme
2 cups (500 ml) ruby port
2 teaspoons (10 ml) finely chopped, fresh
    peeled ginger
Zest of 1 large orange
2 cups (500 ml) mixed berries (such as
    strawberries, blueberries, raspberries and
    blackberries), whatever is market fresh

Salt and pepper to taste

- Season the pork with salt and pepper, sprinkle evenly with rosemary and drizzle with olive oil.

- To make the sauce add the port, thyme, shallot, ginger and orange zest to a medium sized saucepan over medium heat. Bring to a boil then reduce heat to a low simmer. Simmer until reduced by half.

- Strain the liquid into a bowl using a fine mesh strainer. Add the berries to the hot liquid and stir. This will release some juices into the sauce without ruining the tender berries. Season to taste with salt and pepper. Reserve.

- Preheat barbecue with two burners set to medium: 375F (190C), and the other 2 burners set to low: 275F (135C). Oil grill.

- Place the tenderloins directly on the grill over medium-high heat. Cook for 3–4 minutes or until nice golden char marks are achieved. Flip the tenderloin and continue to cook until both sides are nicely charred. Roll tenderloin on its sides to get equal charring all over the loin. This gives more flavour.

- Once the tenderloin is nicely charred move to the low heat side of the barbecue, close lid and cook a further 5–8 minutes, or until an instant read thermometer inserted in the thickest part reads 150F (65C). Turn tenderloins halfway through cooking.

- Remove from grill, tent the pork loosely with foil and let rest 15 minutes.

- Slice and serve with a spoonful of the wild berry sauce.

PLANKED APRICOT DIJON PORK

Most people think salmon on cedar when they think BBQing with plank wood. But a juicy pork roast gets infused with flavour from slow-cooking on a maple plank. Ask your butcher to leave the "fat cap" on the roast when you order it. It will melt once the roast hits the grill and infuse it with flavour. Check out the marinade: Dijon and apricot jam add a killer taste profile to the pork. Serves 6–8

4–5 lb (1.81–2.26 kg) pork loin roast
    with 1/4-inch (5 mm) fat cap

1/4 cup (60 ml) Dijon mustard

1/4 cup (75 ml) plus 1 tablespoon good
    quality apricot jam

1 tablespoon (15 ml) fresh ginger chopped fine

1/4 cup (60 ml) rice wine vinegar

1/4 cup (60 ml) olive oil

Salt and pepper to taste

1 maple plank soaked in cool water
    for 1–2 hours

Have handy a spray bottle filled with water

- In a small bowl mix together Dijon, apricot jam, ginger, rice wine vinegar, olive oil and pepper. Place the pork in a sealable bag and pour the marinade over. Refrigerate overnight.

- Remove pork from marinade and place on tray. Season with salt and pepper.

- Remove one grill on one side of the barbecue. Preheat barbecue to high: 475F–500F (246C-260C) on the side without a grill grate. Preheat the other side to medium-low heat: 325F (162C).

- Place the soaked plank directly over flame (no grate side). Close lid and wait for smoke. Then move the plank over to the medium-low side, place pork on the plank, fat-side up and close lid.

- Slow cook for 1 1/2 hours. Or until a thermometer reads 150–160F (65C–71C) when inserted in the thickest part of the roast. Check the plank every so often for any flare ups and spray with water if they happen.

- Remove from grill, cover loosely with foil and rest for 20 minutes. Carve into thin slices.

PORK PICNIC SHOULDER WITH BLACKBERRY CHIPOTLE GLAZE

Serves 8–10

1 6-lb (2.72 kg) picnic pork shoulder roast,
bone in

Orange Marinade:

1 cup (250 ml) pure unsweetened orange juice

2 tablespoons (30 ml) fresh basil leaves,
stems removed and roughly chopped

2 tablespoons (30 ml) fresh lime juice

2 tablespoons (30 ml) olive oil

2 teaspoons (10 ml) finely chopped fresh garlic

1 teaspoon (5 ml) red pepper flakes

Pepper to taste

Blackberry Chipotle Barbecue Sauce:

1 small Spanish onion, finely chopped

1 lb (454 g) fresh blackberries

2 tablespoons (30 ml) good quality
blackberry jam

3 whole canned chipotle peppers in adobo
sauce roughly chopped

1/4 (60 ml) cup apple cider vinegar

Juice and zest of one large lime

Zest of 1 orange

Salt and pepper to taste

Olive oil for brushing

8–10 soft rolls

2 cups (500 ml) fresh spring mix

6 cups (1.5 liter) apple wood chips 4 cups
(1 liter) soaked in cool water for 1 hour
and drained.

- For the marinade, mix all ingredients together.

- Place the pork in a large sealable baggie and pour over the marinade. Refrigerate for 12 hours.

- To make barbecue sauce, place all ingredients into a medium saucepan over minimum heat and simmer for 15 minutes. Remove from heat.

- Prepare barbecue for smoking over indirect heat: 220F (104C). Leave 2 burners off and 1 burner on high.

- Prepare smoke pouch (see page 37).

- Remove pork from marinade pat dry and season with salt and pepper.

- Adjust your barbecue temperature to 220F (104C). Place a drip pan under the side without heat. Place pork over the drip pan. Close lid.

- Smoke for 1 hour and baste often with the barbecue sauce. Continue to cook for 2 more hours changing the smoke pouch when necessary and basting with the sauce.

- Pork is done when an instant read thermometer inserted in the thickest part of the pork and away from the bone reads 160 F (71C).

- Remove and rest, covered loosely in foil for 20 minutes.

- Carve and serve with sauce on buns with lettuce.

SAUCY RIBS

Ribs are by far one of the most popular and versatile BBQ dishes with end-less permutations of sauces and rubs. Ribs benefit from long slow cooking at low temperature (with or without smoke) which is easier to achieve on the BBQ than it is in your kitchen oven. As always we encourage you to fiddle with the ingredients and come up with your own personal version. Yield: 2 full racks of baby back ribs

2 full sides baby back pork ribs
  approximately 3 lbs each (1.5kg)

Rub:

1/4 cup (60 ml) lightly packed brown sugar

2 tablespoons (30 ml) kosher salt

1 teaspoon (5 ml) freshly grated nutmeg

2 teaspoons (10 ml) ground cinnamon

2 teaspoons (10 ml) mustard powder

1 teaspoon (5 ml) dry thyme leaves

2 teaspoons (10 ml) onion powder

2 teaspoons (10 ml) garlic powder

1 teaspoon (5 ml) ground allspice

2 teaspoons (10 ml) dried sage

2 teaspoons (10 ml) dried oregano

Classic barbecue sauce:

2 tablespoons (30 ml) olive oil

1 medium Spanish onion, small dice

2 tablespoons (30 ml) minced garlic

2 tablespoons (30 ml) jalapeño, seeded
  and chopped fine

1 cup (250 ml) tomato paste

1 cup (250 ml) strong coffee

1/2 cup (125 ml) Worcestershire sauce

1/2 cup (125 ml) apple cider vinegar

Cond't:

- Combine all rub ingredients in a small bowl and mix well.

- Remove the tough connective skin at back of the ribs. Using a pair of pliers or your hands, pull at the white thin skin in one motion to remove.

- Massage the rub over both sides of the pork ribs quite aggressively. Place on a tray and refrigerate overnight.

- To make the sauce, warm oil in a medium sauté pan over high heat for 30 seconds. Add the onion and garlic and cook until the onion is translucent. Add the remaining sauce ingredients and bring to a boil. Reduce heat to low and simmer 15 minutes. Use immediately or chill.

- Prepare 3 smoke pouches (see page 37) by mixing 2 cups (500 ml) of wet chips with 1 cup (250 ml) of the dry and sprinkle each with the dry herb mixture. Mix well.

- Prepare barbecue for indirect smoking by preheating one side to high: 220F (104C) and leaving one side off. Place a drip pan under the grill on the no heat side.

- Place smoke pouch on direct heat and wait for smoke. Once pouch is smoking adjust heat if necessary. Place ribs over the drip pan. Close lid and smoke for 2 1/2 hours, replacing the pouch when smoke dissipates.

Classic barbecue sauce cond't:

1/2 cup (125 ml) lightly packed brown sugar

1/2 cup (125 ml) fresh apple cider

9 cups apple wood chips (2.25 L), 6 cups
(1.5 L) of the chips soaked in cool water
for 1 hour and drained.

1 teaspoon each dried sage, oregano, thyme

- In the last 1/2 hour of cooking, start basting with the sauce. Use it all if you like them saucy, or reserve some for a dipping sauce.

- Ribs will be perfect when you gently tug on some of the flesh and it falls off the bone. Remove ribs, cover loosely with foil and let rest 10–15 minutes.

- Using a sharp knife cut the ribs between the bones.

SAUSAGE WITH CARAMELIZED ONION AND PEPPER

This ain't no ordinary sausage on a bun. First you plump up the tube steak by simmering it in a beer bath along with the onions and red pepper, *then* you grill it. The extra flavour pop comes from the caramelized onions. For this you will need a cast iron skillet. Don't have one? They're inexpensive and are the best at conducting heat and will survive being used on a BBQ's direct heat. Yield: 8 sausage buns

8 mild Italian sausages

4 cups (1 L) ginger beer or beer

4 medium Spanish onions, sliced thin

3 garlic cloves, sliced thin

2 teaspoons (10 ml) mustard seeds

1 teaspoon (5 ml) whole caraway seeds

1 teaspoon (5 ml) whole coriander seeds

3 large red peppers cut into 1/4-inch
  (6-mm) strips

2 tablespoons (30 ml) olive oil

8 crusty sausage buns and your favourite
  mustard

Olive oil for brushing

- Pour the ginger beer or beer in a large skillet over medium high heat, add the onions, garlic and spices and bring to a gentle boil.

- Reduce heat to a low simmer, add the sausage and simmer for 10 minutes.

- Remove sausages from liquid and pat dry. Strain the onion mix and reserve. Discard the poaching liquid.

- Preheat a large cast iron pan on the grill set at medium heat: 350F (175C). Add oil to the pan, heat 1 minute and add the strained onion and garlic slices. Close the lid and cook for 30 minutes, stirring occasionally or until nice and golden brown and caramelized. Add the red peppers and cook a further 10 minutes. Season with salt and pepper, remove from heat and keep warm.

- Once the sausages are cool, brush with olive oil.

- Preheat barbecue to high: 475F–500F (204C-260C). Oil grill, place the sausages on the grill and cook for 10 minutes (approximately 5 minutes per side) or until golden brown.

- Remove from grill and serve the sausage with the warm onion pepper topping on crusty buns with your favourite mustard.

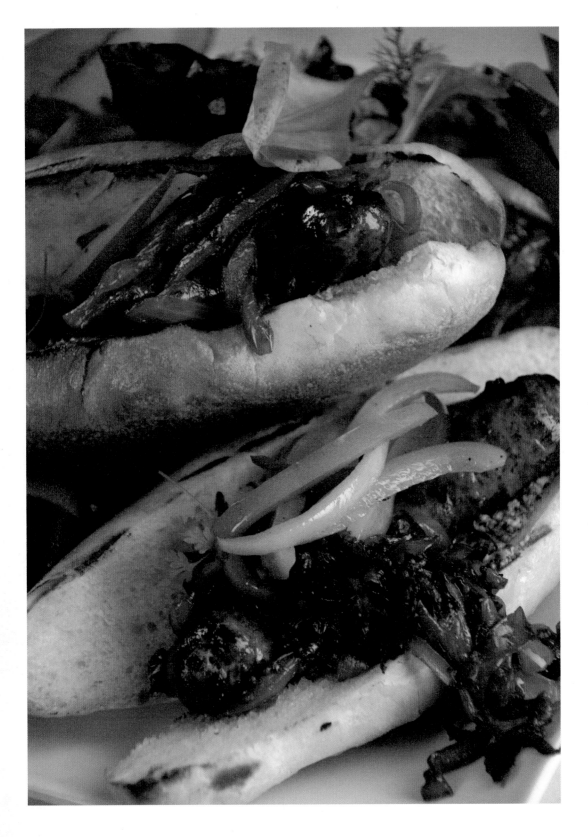

SMOKED PAPAYA PORK BUTT

Pork butt is one of those tough, fatty cuts of pork that magically transforms into tender pull-apart meat when marinated and cooked over low heat for an extended amount of time. We've come up with an interesting and delicious marinade that includes papaya juice, lemon juice and fish sauce. Papaya juice is loaded with enzymes that break down the tough connective tissue in the butt. This one is a winner. Serves 6–8

1 6-lb (2.72 kg) pork butt, bone out

Marinade:

1 tablespoon (15 ml) chopped garlic

2 cups (500 ml) all natural unsweetened
   papaya juice

2 tablespoons (30 ml) fresh lemon juice

1 teaspoon (5 ml) hot sauce

1 teaspoon (5 ml) dried red chili flakes

2 teaspoons (10 ml) dried oregano

2 teaspoons (10 ml) fish sauce

1/2 cup (125 ml) Spanish onion, diced fine

1/4 cup (60 ml) olive oil

Salt and pepper to taste

Additional olive oil for brushing

9 cups (2.25 L) hickory wood chips, 6 cups
   (1.5 liter) of the chips soaked in cool
   water for 1 hour and drained

- In a medium sized bowl whisk together all marinade ingredients excluding the salt.

- Place pork in a heavy duty sealable baggie. Pour marinade over and ensure the pork is evenly covered. Marinate overnight in the refrigerator.

- Remove the pork from the marinade. Drizzle with olive oil and sprinkle with salt and pepper.

- Make 3 smoke pouches (see page 37).

- Prepare barbecue for indirect cooking and smoking. Turn one side of the barbecue on high leaving the other side off. Slide a drip pan under the grill on the side that is off. Place the smoke pouch on the side that is on. Wait for smoke.

- Adjust heat to read 220F (104C). Place pork over drip pan, close lid and allow to slow cook for 5 hours. Change the smoke pouch when the smoke dissipates.

- Remove from the grill, tent with foil for 20–25 minutes. Carve and serve.

SWEET, SMOKY, STICKY SPARERIBS

If you've got kids then these are the ribs for you. Just like the name says they're sweet and sticky and smoky, and we use all the stuff kids love, like ketchup and ballpark mustard and brown sugar. Yep, grown ups love them too. Put the rub on the ribs on Friday night and then leave them smoking on the BBQ all Saturday afternoon while you do other stuff. Doesn't get any easier. Yield: 2 whole racks of ribs

2 full whole racks spareribs

Rub:

1/4 cup (60 ml) brown sugar

3 tablespoons (45 ml) sweet paprika

1 tablespoon (15 ml) kosher salt

2 teaspoons (10 ml) garlic powder

2 teaspoons (10 ml) onion powder

2 teaspoons (10 ml) ground cinnamon

1 teaspoon (5 ml) ground coriander

1 teaspoons (5 ml) cayenne pepper

2 teaspoons (10 ml) mustard powder

1 teaspoon (5 ml) cracked black pepper

Sauce:

1 1/2 cups (375 ml) ketchup

1/4 cup (60 ml) cider vinegar

1/4 cup (60 ml) Worcestershire sauce

1/4 cup (60 ml) brown sugar

2 tablespoons (30 ml) ballpark mustard

1 tablespoon (15 ml) hot sauce

1 tablespoon (15 ml) extra rub seasoning
    from above recipe

Salt and pepper to taste

9 cups (2.25 L) cherry wood chips, 6 cups
    (1.5 L) of the chips soaked in cool water
    for 1 hour and drained.

- Trim the racks of any loose fat and remove tough connective tissue on backside.

- In a small bowl combine all the rub ingredients, reserving 1 tablespoon (15 ml) of the rub for the sauce. Massage rub into meat quite aggressively to tear little micro pockets in the flesh to allow the flavour in. Marinate overnight in the refrigerator.

- For the sauce, whisk together all ingredients in a bowl.

- Prepare barbecue for indirect cooking. Preheat one side to high: 225–250F (107C–121C) and leave the other side off. Place a drip pan under the grill on the side without heat.

- Prepare 3 smoke pouches (see page 37). Place a smoke pouch on direct heat and place the ribs over the drip pan on the side without heat.

- Cook the ribs for 2–3 hours, changing the smoke pouch when smoke dissipates.

- Heavily brush the ribs with sauce and continue to cook a further 45 minutes. Ribs will be done when you can easily pull them from the bone.

- Remove from grill, tent with foil and rest meat for 20 minutes.

- Slice between bones and serve with sauce.

PORK TENDERLOIN WITH A HAWAIIAN FRUIT BBQ SAUCE

Yield: 5 servings

2 whole pork tenderloins trimmed and
   silver skin removed

Sauce:

1 lb (454 g) fresh apricots, pitted and halved

1 lb (454 g) fresh peaches, pitted and
   sliced thin

1 medium can crushed pineapple

1/2 cup (125 ml) applesauce

1 cup (250 ml) white vinegar

1 teaspoon (5 ml) hot sauce

3 tablespoons (45 ml) tomato paste

1 cup (250 ml) firmly packed golden
   brown sugar

2 teaspoons (10 ml) dry mustard

1/2 cup (125 ml) unsalted butter

Juice of 2 limes

Salt and pepper to taste

Olive oil for grilling

- To make the sauce, melt the butter in a large skillet set over medium heat. Add peaches and apricots and sauté for 3–4 minutes until nicely caramelized.

- Add the remaining ingredients except the lime juice and salt and pepper. Stir to combine and reduce heat to low. Simmer for 30 minutes or until the mixture is thickened and coats the back of a spoon.

- Remove from heat and allow to cool. Add the lime juice and season to taste with salt and pepper. Puree in a blender until smooth, and strain.

- Season the pork with salt and pepper and drizzle with olive oil.

- Preheat barbecue. Set two burners to medium high: 375F (190C), and set the other 2 burners to low: 275F (135C). Oil grill and place the tenderloins directly on grill over the medium-high heat.

- Cook for 3–4 minutes or until nice golden char marks are achieved. Flip and continue to cook the pork until both sides are nicely charred. Roll tenderloin on its sides to get equal charring all over the loin. This provides more flavour.

- Once the tenderloin is nicely charred move to the side of the barbecue with low heat setting, close lid and cook a further 5–8 minutes, or until an instant read thermometer inserted in the thickest part reads 150F (65C). Turn the tenderloins halfway through cooking.

- Remove from grill, tent loosely with foil and let rest 15 minutes.

- Slice the pork into medallions and plate. Spoon sauce over top and serve immediately with wild rice salad (see page 192) and grilled veggies.

LAMB

Who decided to describe the taste of lamb as "gamey"? They should be taken out behind the BBQ and paddled. Lamb is **not** a game meat. One goes out into the forest and hunts for game with rifles and dogs and plaid shirts. Have you ever heard of someone hunting for lamb? Lamb does not taste gamey. It tastes like lamb, which is as hard to describe as the taste of an orange or a bacon cheeseburger.

Lamb is rich and textured and complex – definitely not gamey. The taste of lamb varies quite a bit depending on where it's from (way more than beef). In the world of wine, the French call this *"gout du terroire"* or "taste of the earth" depending on where the grape is from. Same goes for lamb, which is enthusiastically consumed from New Zealand to Greece and everywhere in-between. Lamb is also a meat that I like to grill to a medium pink (as opposed to medium rare for beef) as the extra cooking time seems to further develop the flavour without drying it out (I'm referring to grilling cuts here, not those you slow cook).

For lamb on the BBQ, here are the main cuts you need to know about:

CHOPS They come from either the loin or the ribs. The loin chops are by far the most popular and the most expensive. I like to buy a rack and slice between each rib bone. Voila, a whole bunch of rib chops. Either way, you want to grill them medium to medium rare. Have your butcher French the bones. You can also buy shoulder chops but for most people, the loin or rib chops are the way to go.

RACK A whole bunch of ribs with lots of flavour and very juicy. Because they take a bit longer to cook than chops (because of the thickness), I start the rack over direct high heat to get some nice colour and then move it over to the unlit side for indirect cooking. Make sure your butcher removes the silver skin you get sometimes as it will shrink under heat, tightening up the meat.

RIBS Yes the ribs. They're delicious and nobody orders lamb ribs so they are inexpensive. There's a great recipe on page 72.

LOIN Loins are very juicy and lean cuts that cook really quickly (again medium to medium rare) so keep an eye on it. Like the rack, you start a loin off over high heat and then move it over to either indirect cooking or direct low-heat cooking. Slice the loin into medallions before serving.

LEG Got to love a leg of lamb. It's a versatile cut that works with both rubs and marinades. It has some nice marbling so you get lots of flavour and cooked properly, you get a nice crispy skin and some well done slices on the outside moving towards medium or medium rare right next to the bone so there's something for everyone. Speaking of which, I often go on about cooking bone-in whenever possible. That's true with a leg of lamb as it adds additional flavour. But this is one cut where I would encourage you to try it boned, butterflied and on the rotisserie at least once. Don't worry, your friendly butcher will be pleased to do it all for you in advance if you call him. There are very few BBQ sights and smells as wonderful as a whole leg of lamb slathered in herbs and slowly turning on the spit. It's enough to make a guy cry.

LAMB BURGER There are all sorts of trimmings left when your butcher carves up a lamb carcass. There's also meat on the ribs that will be removed and either ground up for burgers or used to make sausages. Typically the ground meat comes from the leg or the shoulder (not as much fat as other cuts) and makes for an excellent change from your go-to beef patties. There is more fat in lamb than in beef so just watch out for flare ups.

KABOBS Sometimes you'll find nice cubes of lamb meat for sale (referred to as stewing cubes or stewing lamb). They come from less tender bits and are therefore way less expensive if you are feeding a whole bunch of people. The secret here is to marinate the lamb in order to tenderize it (but you knew that already, didn't you?) Check out all the marinades in the final chapter for some ideas.

SHANK This is probably my personal favourite. It's a tougher cut and requires marinating or basting and definitely slow cooking (sometimes smoking if you're so inclined). But when you're done the shank is tender fall-off-the-bone meat with a rich deep lamb flavour.

Whichever cut you go with, try incorporating more lamb into your BBQ rotation. Oh yeah, in case you haven't read the other chapters, always tent your meat with foil after it comes off the grill. Always. Don't make me come over there and take your BBQ tongs away from you.

GRILLED LAMB CHOPS WITH MINT PESTO

Mint pesto on grilled lamb chops rocks. It's the perfect combo. Not that cloying mint jelly your Gram dolloped on her overcooked lamb. This is fresh tangy mint pesto with a touch of heat from the chili flakes. The pesto here doubles as a marinade. Serve the chops with some couscous studded with dried cranberries and pour yourself a glass of slightly chilled Zinfandel. Nice. Ask your butcher to French (fancy term for clean) the bones for you. Serves 6

3 full racks of lamb, bones Frenched and
   cut into 2 bone chops
Salt and pepper to taste
Olive oil for brushing

Pesto:
1 1/2 cups (375 ml) mint leaves, stems
   removed
2/3 cup (165 ml) fresh parsley leaves
1/4 cup (60 ml) pine nuts or walnuts
Pinch of red pepper flakes
2 teaspoons (10 ml) chopped garlic
2 teaspoons (10 ml) lemon zest
1 tablespoon (15 ml) fresh lemon juice
1/3 cup (83 ml) olive oil

- Puree all the pesto ingredients except the oil in a blender or food processor until smooth. Gradually add the oil through the feed tube. Puree until an even consistency. Reserve 1/2 cup (125 ml) for basting and dipping.

- Place the cut chops in a sealable plastic bag. Evenly coat with pesto and marinate for 5 hours in the refrigerator.

- Remove lamb from marinade, brush with olive oil and season both sides with salt and pepper.

- Wipe the marinade off the bones to prevent burning.

- Preheat barbecue to medium-high: 375F (190C). Oil grill.

- Place chops directly on the grill for approximately 4–5 minutes per side for medium rare or less depending on how you like your lamb. Using tongs, flip the lamb and brush with the reserved marinade on the cooked side. Continue to cook for 4 minutes.

- Remove from grill and loosely cover with foil for 10 minutes to rest the meat.

- Serve with remaining pesto.

When grilling lamb on the bone you can cover the bones with foil to prevent burning.

LAMB SOUVLAKI

Souvlaki is sort of Greek fast food. We serve this lamb version up on pita with some creamy garlicky store-bought tzatziki sauce for a quick and easy dinner. Make sure you trim the fat off the lamb cubes to avoid flare ups.

Yield: about 8–10 kabobs

2 lbs (907 g)lamb loin trimmed of fat,
   cut into 1 inch squares

Marinade:
1/4 cup (60 ml) fresh lemon juice
3 tablespoons (45 ml) olive oil
1 1/2 tablespoons (22.5 ml) fresh oregano
1 tablespoon (15 ml) fresh chopped garlic
1/4 cup (60 ml) grated Spanish onion
Pepper

1 cup (250 ml) store-bought or
   homemade tzatziki sauce
Olive oil for brushing
Tin foil
Salt and pepper
6 pita or 15 mini pita bread
10 bamboo skewers soaked in
   cool water for 30 minutes

- In a medium bowl combine marinade ingredients and mix well.

- Add the lamb cubes to the marinade and coat all the lamb. Place in a sealable baggie and marinate overnight in the refrigerator.

- Remove lamb from the marinade and thread 2–3 cubes onto each skewer. Season the cubes with salt and pepper.

- Preheat barbecue for direct grilling at high: 475F–500F (246C–260C). Oil grill.

- Place lamb on grill and place foil underneath the exposed wood of the skewers this will prevent the sticks from charring.

- Cook for 2 minutes per side or until nice char marks are achieved.

- Remove lamb from grill and serve in pita bread with tzatziki sauce.

ROTISSERIE LEG OF LAMB VERDE

Hey, you get to break out the rotisserie for this one. I love the rotisserie but it doesn't get used so much by most folk. Normally I'm a medium-rare kind of guy but like my lamb cooked medium. I find it brings out more of that wonderful complex lamb flavour. Check out the ingredients in the marinade – all classic lamb matches in one bowl. The wine in the drip pan adds an extra perfume to the meat while it's cooking. Grilled asparagus and potatoes are perfect with this, along with a slightly chilled Pinot Noir. Serves 6–8

3 lb (1.4 kg) boneless leg of lamb, tied

Marinade:

Juice and zest of 2 lemons

1 cup (250 ml) lightly packed fresh basil,
   stems removed

1/2 cup (125 ml) fresh mint leaves,
   stems removed

2 tablespoons (30 ml) fresh oregano leaves,
   stems removed

1 cup (250 ml) Italian flat leaf parsley,
   stems removed

4 cloves garlic

2 tablespoons (30 ml) Dijon mustard

2 tablespoons (30 ml) capers, drained

4 anchovy fillets

1/2 cup (125 ml) olive oil

Cracked pepper and salt to taste

Drip pan:

2 cups (500 ml) white wine

1 bunch mixed herbs such as oregano,
   thyme, parsley

- Pulse the garlic in a blender or processor; add the remaining marinade ingredients and puree until smooth. Season to taste with salt and pepper.

- Reserve 1/2 cup (125 ml) of the marinade for drizzling over the lamb when it is finished.

- Place lamb leg in a large sealable container or baggie. Pour the marinade over the leg evenly and marinate overnight in the refrigerator, turning once or twice to coat.

- Preheat barbecue for indirect cooking, rotisserie heat. Place 2 burners on and leave the middle burner off. Adjust temperature to 325F (162C) and place a drip pan on the middle burner.

- Remove lamb from the marinade and bring to room temperature. This will promote even cooking and help achieve the perfect cooked temperature from outside to inside.

- Secure the lamb on rotisserie in centre of the rod, following manufacturer's instructions. Tighten the bolts. Position lamb in centre of the barbecue over drip pan. Place the wine and herbs in the drip pan.

- Turn rotisserie on and adjust the counter weight to ensure even rotation.

- Cook the lamb 1 – 1 1/2 hours or 15 minutes per pound or to when an instant read thermometer inserted in the thickest part reads 125F (51C) for medium rare.

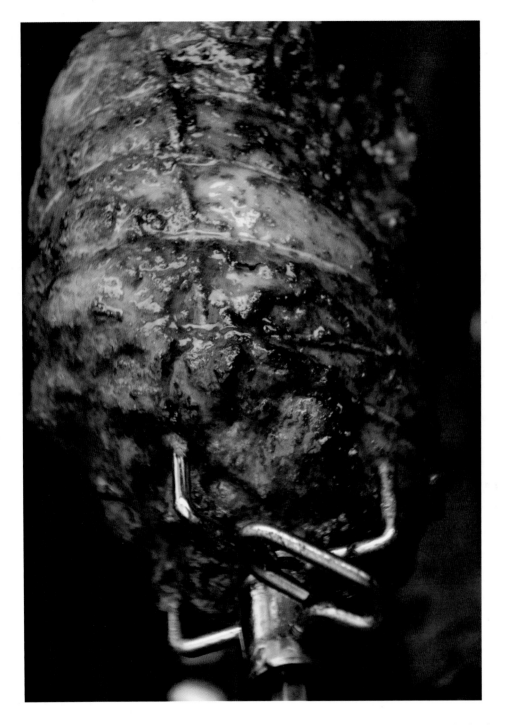

- Check the roast regularly and baste with pan juices collected in the drip pan.

- Remove from grill and tent with foil for 20–25 minutes.

- Remove the prongs and slice the lamb to desired thickness. Serve with crusty bread and the reserved marinade.

SPICY TANDOORI LAMB RIBS

That's right . . . lamb ribs. Most people think pork or beef when they think ribs but wait till you try these. They're smaller and don't take anywhere near as long to cook. Also, they're pretty inexpensive as most butchers end up taking the meat off the ribs and making sausage out of it because nobody orders them. Watch your butcher's face light up when you walk in and ask for a bunch of lamb ribs. Yield: 1 rack

1 rack lamb ribs, trimmed, approximately
  4 lbs (1.81 kg)

Marinade:
Juice of 1 lemon
2 teaspoons (10 ml) ground black pepper
2 cloves of garlic, minced
1 tablespoon (15 ml) freshly grated ginger
2 teaspoons (10 ml) ground coriander
1 teaspoon (5 ml) garam masala spice mix
1 teaspoon (5 ml) ground cayenne
1 teaspoon (5 ml) ground turmeric
2 teaspoons (10 ml) hot curry paste
1 cup (250 ml) plain yogurt

Salt and pepper to taste
Olive oil for brushing

- In a medium bowl mix together all marinade ingredients until well combined. Reserve 1/2 cup for basting.

- Place the lamb ribs in a large sealable plastic bag. Pour the marinade over and evenly coat. Refrigerate overnight.

- Remove from fridge and place ribs on tray. Drizzle with oil and season with salt and pepper.

- Prepare barbecue for indirect low and slow cooking: 220F (104C). Leave one burner on high and the remaining burners off. Oil grill.

- Place a drip pan under the side without heat. Place the lamb over the drip pan (indirect heat) close lid and cook for 1 hour.

- After 1 hour begin to turn and baste the ribs with the reserved marinade. Continue to cook until a nice crust is achieved and ribs are fork tender, approximately 45 minutes to 1 hour.

- Remove from grill, tent with foil and allow the lamb to rest 30 minutes. Carve between the bones and serve with cool yogurt if desired.

POULTRY

We eat a lot of poultry and chicken. The average
North American puts away about 85 pounds
(50 kilograms) of the stuff every year.
But not all chickens are created equal . . .

What species of chicken is your chicken? Google "types of chicken" and you'll learn there are at least 20 different varieties raised in North America. In France and Italy (and elsewhere in Europe I imagine), chickens are often sold by their varietal names. Many regions are as proud and as protective of their local poultry as they are of their wine. But here, we just go into a store and ask for chicken. It's kind of like going into a fishmonger and saying "Hey, I'd like some fish please." We seem to be more interested in the grade and quality of a bird than its provenance. So here's a quick primer:

Buying a chicken

At the top of the pecking order (pardon the pun) is your organic bird. Organic means a chicken that has been fed nothing but organically grown soybean and grain and has been raised without the use of antibiotics, growth hormones or any other drugs or chemicals. Organic birds are generally not "free range" so as to ensure the chicken doesn't scarf back the odd toxic worm.

Free range and grain fed birds are considered the next best thing, although if you have visions of your free range bird frolicking happily in a field of clover, think again. The avian flu scare has forced farmers to move their birds inside for the most part. They still get to run around, albeit in large open barns.

Next you've got your run-of-the-mill everyday chicken, raised in the dark, squished together in tight pens and fed all sorts of nasty things to make them plump and tasteless. By the way, the difference between a free range bird and one that's been raised inhumanely is about a buck a pound. You decide if it's worth the splurge.

Chickens get the once-over by health inspectors and are graded A, B or C. You want an A chicken.

Then there's size. You've got your broiler/fryer (7–13 weeks old, 1–2 kg), roaster (3–5 months, 2–4 kg) and then something called stewer which are 10 months old at least and should probably be pulling rickshaws rather than being eaten.

And if that weren't enough to confuse the average poultry purchaser, you've got the choice between water-cooled and air-cooled birds. What does this mean, you ask? Well, once the bird has been dispatched, it has to be cooled before being packaged or chopped up. This can be done in either a super-cooled room (air cooled) or being immersed in cold water (water cooled). Which is better? There is apparently no nutritional difference but most chicken connoisseurs prefer the air-chilled variety.

Finally, there's the chicken's gender. Girl chickens are called pullets or hens. Boy birds are cockerels or cocks. And then there's the capon. What's a capon? Well a capon is a castrated cock. Seriously. I'm not making this up. You see, cutting off boy chickens' family jewels makes them more docile and non-aggressive (draw your own conclusions here) and less likely to develop male characteristics like fighting, hitting on girl chickens, excessive flatulence and watching sports for hours on end.

Confused? Thinking of ordering pizza now? Chill. This is where your ongoing relationship with a good reputable butcher comes in handy. When you earn your living selling meat and only meat you make sure it's good quality. Talk to your butcher, tell him what you want, then have BBQ'd chicken.

Your chicken and your BBQ

Listen, nobody likes a nice breast more than me, but I'd like to put a plug in for the other chicken choices. I think chicken thighs have way more flavour than the breasts. It's a darker meat and there are bones which automatically means more flavour. And if you've only ever had deep-fried chicken wings at your local sports bar, wait till you try BBQing them.

If you are going to go with the breast then please consider bone-in and skin on. Bone means flavour and so does skin. If you're watching your weight, take the skin off *after* the grilling.

But really the best way to cook a chicken is whole, either on the rotisserie or on the grill using indirect heat.

Whatever you do, don't forget to tent your poultry with tin foil once it comes off the BBQ. This allows the meat to relax and the juices to seep back into all the meat. Trust me.

ASIAN CHICKEN IN LETTUCE LEAVES

Lettuce leaves are a great alternative to carb-heavy breads and buns on which to place your BBQ treats. This is glazed grilled chicken wrapped in lettuce leaves and served with a peanut dipping sauce. Yield: 6 servings

For the glaze:

2 tablespoons (30 ml) peanut oil

2 tablespoons (30 ml) grated ginger

1 1/2 tablespoons (23 ml) chopped garlic

1/4 cup (60 ml) soy sauce

3/4 cup (190 ml) honey of good quality

Juice of 2 lemons

1 teaspoon (5 ml) freshly ground
    black pepper

For the sauce:

2 tablespoons (15 ml) peanut oil

1/2 cup (125 ml) fine diced white onion

2 garlic cloves, minced

1 1/2 teaspoons (7.5 ml) chili paste

1/2 teaspoon (2.5 ml) curry powder

2 teaspoons (10 ml) kosher salt

1/4 cup (60 ml) smooth all natural
    peanut butter

1/4 cup (60 ml) coconut milk

2 teaspoons (10 ml) rice wine vinegar

2 tablespoons (30 ml) brown sugar

1/4 cup (60 ml) coarsely chopped roasted,
    unsalted peanuts

1/4 cup (60 ml) boiling water

For the glaze:

- Heat the oil in a medium saucepan set over medium-high heat. Add the ginger and garlic and cook while stirring until soft without browning. Stir in the soy sauce, lemon juice and honey. Remove from heat; add the black pepper and cool.

For the peanut sauce:

- Heat oil in a medium skillet over medium heat.

- Add the onions and garlic and cook until translucent, about 3 minutes. Add the chili paste and curry powder and stir to combine. Stir in the peanut butter, coconut milk, rice vinegar, brown sugar and 2 tablespoons of the warm water. Let simmer for 1–2 minutes or until the peanut butter dissolves.

- Add 2 tablespoons (30 ml) of the peanuts to the sauce and transfer it to a blender. Blend until smooth, adding 2–4 tablespoons of boiling water to help the sauce emulsify. Transfer to a bowl and garnish with remaining peanuts.

For the chicken:

8 boneless, skinless chicken thighs, cut in half

1 bunch fresh cilantro, washed and dried

1 bunch fresh mint leaves

1 head of bibb lettuce

Vegetable oil for brushing

16 bamboo skewers soaked in cool water
   for 30 minutes

For the chicken:

- Preheat barbecue to medium high: 375F (190C). Oil grill.

- Thread the chicken onto skewers and place on a flat baking tray. Brush with oil and season with salt and pepper.

- Place chicken on the oiled grill and grill for 3–4 minutes on one side and flip. Brush with the glaze and continue to cook while basting until the chicken is cooked through and golden brown.

- Remove chicken and place on a platter with cilantro, mint and lettuce. Place two pieces of chicken in lettuce leaves with cilantro and mint and roll loosely.

- Serve with peanut sauce.

BEER CAN CHICKEN

Beer can chicken has become all the rage amongst the BBQ set because a) it's easy to do, b) it tastes delicious, and c) it looks funny. We've spiced our version up by adding a Jamaican jerk marinade so you get the "brewski effect" (that would be the beer evaporating in the can and moistening the bird from inside) plus a nice spice on the crispy skin. Serve this one up with a nice spud salad and some grilled asparagus . . . and of course some excellent chilled beer. Yield: 3–4 servings

1 whole chicken rinsed and patted dry,
   5 lb (2.2kg)

Jamaican Marinade:

3 scallions, chopped fine

2 teaspoons (10 ml) ground allspice

1 1/2 teaspoons (7.5 ml) cinnamon

1/2 teaspoon (2.5 ml) ground cloves

1/2 teaspoon (2.5 ml) nutmeg

Splash of soy sauce

Juice of 2 limes

1 tablespoon (15 ml) finely chopped
   fresh ginger

1/4 cup (60 ml) vegetable oil

1 tallboy beer, can covered in foil

- Combine all the ingredients for the marinade in a blender and puree to a smooth consistency.

- Place chicken in a large sealable baggie and pour the marinade over. Swoosh the baggie to ensure the chicken is evenly coated. Marinate in the refrigerator for 6–8 hours.

- Remove from marinade. Discard marinade.

- Prepare barbecue for indirect cooking at medium high: 375F (190C). Leave one burner off and place a drip pan under the grill on the side that is off.

- Remove half of the beer from the can by pouring it in a glass and drinking it.

- Cover the can with foil but leave the top uncovered. This so you don't get paint from the can on your chicken. Place can on the grill over indirect heat. Carefully lower the chicken onto the beer can. Position the legs so as to balance the chicken.

- Close lid and cook over indirect heat until an instant read thermometer when inserted in the thickest part of the bird reads 165F–170F (74C–76C).

- Using dry towels carefully remove the chicken from the barbecue. Cover with foil and allow to rest for 15–20 minutes. At that point remove the chicken from the beer can.

- Carve and serve.

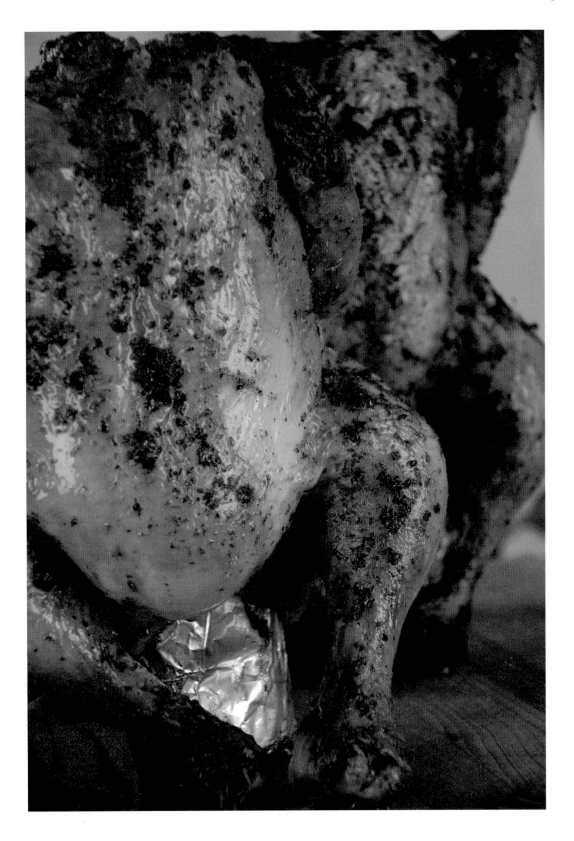

BRICK CHICKEN

Chicken isn't flat and even, like a steak or a pork tenderloin. It has lots of bumps and ups and downs which sometimes makes for uneven cooking. Solution? Flatten the chicken underneath a brick . . . covered in tin foil, of course. Added bonus? Super crispy skin. Yield: 6 servings

6 half chicken breasts, skin on, boneless

Rub:

2 teaspoons (10 ml) ground cumin

1 teaspoon (5 ml) ground coriander

1 teaspoon (5 ml) cinnamon

1 teaspoon (5 ml) red chili pepper flakes

1 teaspoon (5 ml) salt

1 teaspoon (5 ml) fresh ground pepper

Marinade:

2 tablespoons (30 ml) olive oil

1 tablespoon (15 ml) minced fresh garlic

3 tablespoons (45 ml) fresh chopped
   cilantro leaves

3 limes, zested and juiced

4 bricks covered with foil

Oil for brushing

- Combine all ingredients for the rub and mix until combined.

- Rinse chicken well and pat dry. Place on a baking tray and massage rub into chicken aggressively, to tear the flavour into the meat.

- Place in a sealable baggie and pour in the marinade ingredients. Marinate for 1 hour in the refrigerator.

- Preheat grill to medium high: 375F (190F). Oil grill.

- Place the chicken breast skin-side down on a diagonal, and place the foil-covered bricks evenly over chicken.Cook for 2–3 minutes, lift the bricks and give chicken a quarter turn. Replace bricks and continue to cook a further 2–3 minutes.

- Flip the chicken, and continue to cook a further 5–6 minutes, again rotating the breasts a quarter turn after a few minutes. Chicken is cooked when it is slightly firm to the touch and juices run clear.

- Remove bricks. Allow meat to rest under foil for 10 minutes.

CLASSIC BBQ CHICKEN

Sometimes you want comfort food that reminds you of the good old days and BBQ chicken fits the bill. You can bump the garlic and any or all of the spices depending on your palate. Ask your friendly neighbourhood butcher to cut the chicken up for you (try getting that service at a superstore). This is excellent with the Spinach & Cashew Salad on page 184. Serves 3

1 whole 4 lb (1.81 kg) chicken, cut into parts

2 tablespoons (30 ml) olive oil for brushing

2 tablespoons (30 ml) fresh oregano

Salt and pepper

Sauce:

2 tablespoons (30 ml) vegetable oil

1 tablespoon (15 ml) chopped garlic

1 cup (250 ml) yellow onion, finely chopped

2 teaspoons (10 ml) chili powder

2 teaspoons (10 ml) mustard powder

1 teaspoon (5 ml) Spanish paprika

Pinch of cayenne

2 cups (500 ml) crushed tomatoes

1 cup (250 ml) ginger beer

1/4 cup (60 ml) molasses

3 tablespoons (45 ml) Worcestershire

3 tablespoons (45 ml) cider vinegar

- To make the sauce, warm oil in a large skillet set over medium heat, add the onion and garlic and sauté until onion is translucent. Add all the remaining ingredients and reduce heat to low. Simmer for 25 minutes, stirring occasionally. Remove from heat and cool.

- Rinse chicken, pat dry and place on a tray. Season with salt, pepper and oregano and drizzle with olive oil.

- Preheat grill for direct grilling over medium: 350F (176C). Oil grill.

- Place the chicken on the grill skin-side down. Start with the drumsticks and thighs, cook for 5 minutes then add the breasts and wings. Grill, turning once or twice, for 10 minutes.

- Brush with the sauce and continue to grill, turning occasionally, approximately another 10 minutes. Chicken is done when the juices run clear.

- Remove from grill, tent loosely with foil for 10–15 minutes.

GRILLED CHICKEN STICKS WITH PLUM SAUCE

Slice up some ordinary chicken breasts, marinate them, stick 'em on skewers and BBQ. Instant party. Serve with this killer homemade plum sauce. Do *not* skip the mint in the marinade as it really adds a kick to the aftertaste. This is perfect eating-standing-up-food for a backyard party. You can even put the chicken in the marinade in the morning if you'd like and take them out of the fridge 15 minutes or so before BBQing. Yield: 12–14 chicken sticks

4 large chicken breasts, skinless and
   boneless

2 tablespoons (30 ml) olive oil

2 teaspoons (10 ml) lemon zest

2 tablespoons (30 ml) fresh chopped mint

2 teaspoons (10 ml) finely chopped garlic

Salt and pepper to taste

Basting and dipping plum sauce:

3/4 cup (180 ml) good quality plum jam

2 tablespoons (30 ml) fresh lime juice

1 tablespoon (15 ml) rice wine vinegar

2 teaspoons (10 ml) minced ginger

1 tablespoon (15 ml) honey

1 teaspoon (5 ml) finely chopped garlic

3 tablespoons (45 ml) sesame seeds,
   lightly toasted

15 6-inch skewers soaked in cool water
   for 30 minutes prior to grilling

- Cut the chicken lengthwise along the breast into 3/4-inch strips. It doesn't matter if some are shorter; but cooking will be uneven if thickness differs.

- Place chicken in a plastic bag, drizzle with olive oil, mint, lemon zest, garlic and pepper. Toss to evenly coat and marinate in the refrigerator for 1–4 hours.

- Remove from marinade. Thread chicken onto bamboo sticks making sure to cover the tip of skewer with chicken. (To prevent burning tip of the skewer).

- Place on a tray and season with salt (you didn't add this earlier as the salt would have pulled moisture from the already lean chicken breast).

- Combine all the ingredients for the sauce in a small pot and bring to a simmer over low heat. Let simmer 5 minutes.

- Bring 1/2 of a cup the sauce, and sesame seeds to the barbecue with a basting brush along with the skewers on a tray.

- Preheat barbecue to medium: 350F (176C) for direct grilling. Oil grill.

- Place chicken on the grill and slide a piece of foil under the end of the sticks (to prevent any burning). Cook for 3 minutes or until nice golden char marks are achieved. Flip chicken, baste with the sauce and continue to cook until it is golden on both sides and no longer pink in the centre.

- Right before you remove from the grill baste the other side with the plum sauce and sprinkle with sesame seeds.

- Serve with the reserved sauce.

GRILLED CRISPY QUAIL WITH BLOOD ORANGE SAUCE

Blood oranges are tart and have that beautiful deep red colour that makes for a stunning sauce. Your butcher will debone the quail for you. I keep the bones and make an intense stock from them the same way you would with chicken bones. Yield: 6 as an appetizer

6 whole quail, deboned, skin on

Marinade:

1 cup (250 ml) red wine

2/3 cup (165 ml) blood orange (or regular)

1 1/2 tablespoons (22.5 ml) chopped shallots

3 juniper berries

1 bay leaf

1 sprig of fresh thyme

1/4 cup (60 ml) olive oil

Sauce:

6 blood oranges

2 lemons

2 tablespoons (30 ml) sugar

1 cup (250 ml) port

2 cups (250 ml) brown veal stock

1 shallot, minced fine

1 bunch fresh thyme

1/2 cup (125 ml) unsalted cold butter
*   cut into 1-inch (1.6 cm) pieces*

Salt and pepper

Salad:

2 cups (500 ml) watercress, cleaned

1/2 cup (125 ml) crumbled goat cheese

Quail is very lean and doesn't take kindly to overcooking. It's best – and safe – to cook to medium

- Place quail, single layer, in a large, shallow dish. Combine all marinade ingredients in a bowl and pour over quail. Cover and refrigerate for 4 hours.

- To make sauce, zest the skins of the oranges and lemons, place in a small saucepan with the sugar and enough water just to cover. Boil until the sugar begins to caramelize. Strain liquid, reserving zest. Rinse the zest under cool water briefly. Set aside.

- Squeeze juice from the oranges and place in a medium saucepan. Add the port, shallot, thyme and veal stock. Simmer 15 minutes then strain over a bowl.

- Place this liquid back into the pot and simmer over low heat until 1 cup (250 ml) remains. Whisk in the butter, one piece at a time to slightly thicken the sauce. Season to taste with salt and pepper and keep the sauce warm until ready to serve.

- Preheat barbecue to medium-high: 375F (190C). Oil grill. Remove quail from marinade, brush with oil and season with salt and pepper.

- Place quail directly on grill and cook until the skin is golden brown and crisp, about 4–5 minutes. Flip the quail and cook the other side of the bird about 1 minute just to sear the meat.

- Remove from barbecue, cover with foil loosely and rest meat for 5 minutes.

- Arrange watercress on plates and sprinkle with goat cheese. Cut each quail in half lengthwise and place on greens. Spoon sauce over the plate and sprinkle with the reserved orange and lemon zest.

CHICKEN LEGS IN AN HERB PASTE MARINADE

This marinade recipe fairly screams summer and works just as well with chicken breasts or a nice pork tenderloin or roast. Serve with grilled potatoes and asparagus along with an herbaceous white wine like a Sauvignon Blanc.

Serves 4–6

6 chicken legs, skin on

1/4 cup (60 ml) fresh rosemary, leaves only

1 tablespoon (15 ml) fresh oregano leaves

2 tablespoons (30 ml) fresh thyme leaves

6–8 cloves fresh garlic peeled and
    roughly chopped

2 tablespoons (30 ml) olive oil

Zest of 1 orange

Zest of 1 lemon

2 teaspoons (10 ml) orange juice

2 teaspoons (10 ml) lemon juice

1 teaspoon (5 ml) kosher salt

1 teaspoon (5 ml) freshly ground
    black pepper

- For the marinade, place all the ingredients in a food processor and process until well blended. Store in an airtight container and refrigerate till ready to use.

- Pat the chicken legs dry and smear with the marinade. Place the chicken in a sealable plastic bag and put in the fridge for at least 3 hours

- Preheat barbecue to medium high: 375F (190C). Oil grill.

- Wipe the legs clean of any excess marinade. Place chicken on the grill and cook for 6–7 minutes per side or until chicken has golden brown char marks and is cooked through.

- Remove chicken from grill, cover loosely with foil and let rest for 10 minutes.

- Serve immediately.

GRILLED TURKEY BURGERS WITH PINEAPPLE SALSA

Worried about Little Johnny eating too much red meat? Slip one of these in front of him and he'll never talk hamburger again. The pineapple salsa works great with a nice piece of grilled fish as well. Yield: 6 burgers

3 lbs (1.36 kg) ground turkey

Burger mix:

1/4 cup (60 ml) chopped minced green onion

2 teaspoons (10 ml) minced ginger

2 tablespoons (30 ml) chopped basil

Salt and pepper

Oil for brushing

6 soft buns

Optional garnishes: lettuce, red onion,
    and mayonnaise

Salsa:

1/2 pineapple, cored and cut into
    1/4-inch cubes

1 red bell pepper cut into 1/4-inch dice

2 scallions, sliced thin

2 tablespoons (30 ml) small dice red onion

1/2 jalapeno, minced (optional)

2 tablespoons (30 ml) chopped cilantro leaves

1 tablespoon (15 ml) fresh lime juice

Salt and pepper

Oil for brushing

- In a medium bowl mix together all ingredients for the burgers. Using your hands gently form the burgers into 6 patties about 3/4-inch thick. Take care not to handle the meat too much as the temperature of the turkey should be kept as cold as possible at all times.

- Drizzle both sides of the burgers with oil and season with salt and pepper. Refrigerate for 30 minutes to set up.

- To make salsa combine all ingredients in a medium bowl.

- Preheat barbecue to medium: 350–375F (175C–190C). Oil grill well.

- Place burgers on grill and cook 5–6 minutes per side, or until turkey is cooked through and nice char marks are achieved.

- Serve on soft buns with pineapple salsa and other garnishes.

HIGH AND FAST SUICIDE WINGS

These wings are more than just stupid hot, my friend. These wings have a deep and complex taste profile thanks to the molasses, beer, garlic and two vinegars. You can just go with one of the vinegars if you don't have both – just double-up on the quantity. Adjust the level of heat to find your own suicide threshold. Yield: 20 whole wings

20 whole chicken wings ("drumette" and
* "wingette" attached) rinsed and patted dry*

Sauce:

1/2 cup (125 ml) unseasoned rice vinegar

1/2 cup (125 ml) apple cider vinegar

2 teaspoons (10 ml) ground coriander

1/2 teaspoon (2.5 ml) ground cloves

1/2 teaspoon (2.5 ml) ground allspice berries

1 medium onion, diced fine

2 teaspoons (10 ml) minced garlic

1/2 cup (125 ml) lightly packed brown sugar

2 tablespoons (30 ml) blackstrap molasses

2 teaspoons (10 ml) Worcestershire sauce

1/2 bottle dark beer

1/4 cup (60 ml) chipotle chili in adobo
* sauce, minced*

1 tablespoon (15 ml) ground chili paste
* (optional for extra heat)*

2 cups (500 ml) crushed tomatoes

Salt and pepper

- Rinse wings and pat dry.

- Combine all ingredients for the sauce in a saucepan. Set the pan over high heat and bring to a boil. Reduce heat to low and simmer 20 minutes. Remove from heat and cool.

- Place wings in a sealable plastic bag with all but 1 cup of the sauce and marinate in the refrigerator for 4 hours.

- Preheat barbecue to medium: 350F (176C). Oil grill.

- Place wings on grill and cook 10–15 minutes per side or until crispy and cooked through.

- Serve with extra sauce.

HONEY MUSTARD CHICKEN DRUMSTICKS

I don't know who first decided that honey and mustard would be an excellent BBQ combo but whoever it was deserves a medal. This is a super simple recipe – perfect for a weekday night BBQ dinner when you're jammed for time. As always, adjust the recipe to suit your personal tastes. I like way more garlic than we call for here. Yield: 12 drumsticks

12 fresh chicken drumsticks, skin on, rinsed
and patted dry
Oil for brushing

Marinade:

1/2 cup (125 ml) liquid honey

1/4 cup (60 ml) Dijon mustard

1 teaspoon (5 ml) mustard seeds

2 teaspoons (10 ml) chopped garlic

Juice and zest of 1 lemon

2 tablespoons (30 ml) olive oil

Salt and pepper to taste

- In a medium bowl, whisk together all marinade ingredients. Reserve 1/4 cup (60 ml) for basting later.

- Place rinsed chicken in a large sealable plastic bag. Pour the marinade over chicken and swoosh the bag so all the legs are coated with the marinade. Marinate 4 hours in the refrigerator.

- Prepare barbecue for indirect medium heat: 350F (175C) leaving 2 burners on and 2 burners off. Oil the grill on the off-side.

- Place chicken on grill over the burners that are off. Turn every 3–4 minutes, brushing with the reserved marinade, for approximately 15–20 minutes or until chicken skin is golden brown and cooked through or when juices run clear when poked in the thickest part of the drumstick.

- Remove from grill and let rest 5 minutes.

LEMON CHICKEN ON A SPIT

A slow roasting whole chicken lazily spinning on a BBQ rotisserie late on a sunny Saturday afternoon . . . some decent tunes playing . . . a cold beverage in Chef's hand . . . maybe a little Frisbee-fetch with the pooch . . . that distinct chicken aroma wafting over the fence into the neighbour's backyard . . . the neighbour distracting you with a phone call and jumping over the fence to steal the chicken while you're inside . . . the cops coming . . . the tear gas and SWAT team . . . jailhouse tats and then parole . . . good times. On second thought, just invite the neighbours over for dinner. Serves 6

2 whole chickens, 3–4 lb (1.36–1.81 kg) each,
   rinsed and patted dry

2 tablespoons (30 ml) room temperature
   unsalted butter

Oil for brushing

Marinade:

Juice of 4 lemons

1 cup (250 ml) frozen lemonade from
   concentrate, defrosted

1 1/2 tablespoons (22.5 ml) finely
   chopped garlic

1/2 cup (125 ml) fresh cilantro or fresh basil

1/2 cup (125 ml) vegetable oil or
   any neutral flavoured oil

Salt and pepper to taste

**To truss a bird, fold wings close to body.
Tie legs together with long piece of butcher's twine. Turn bird over, pull twine up
and under neck. Tie, and trim ends of
twine.**

- Combine the marinade ingredients in a small bowl.

- Place the chicken in a large sealable baggie and pour marinade over. Swoosh ingredients in bag to evenly coat the chicken. Refrigerate for 30 minutes.

- Remove chicken from marinade. Rub under and over the skin with room temperature butter.

- Season with salt and pepper and truss the chicken so it doesn't flop about. See below.

- Preheat barbecue to medium-low: 325F (162C).

- Slide one of the prongs onto far end of the spit facing centre; slide on the chicken, running spit through the cavity, legs first. Secure legs to prong.

- Slide on second chicken headfirst. Lodge chickens tightly together. Slide on final prong to attach to the chicken legs. Reposition chicken to centre of the spit. Tighten bolts on prongs. Secure counter weight and adjust if necessary.

- Place 1–2 drip pans on grill rack in centre. Attach spit to the motor and turn on power. Close lid and cook chicken 20 minutes per pound or to when a thermometer in the thickest part reads 165F (73C).

- Frequently baste with the drippings in the drip pan.

- Remove chicken, let rest, covered in foil for 15–20 minutes. Use heatproof barbecue gloves to unscrew the bolts. Carve.

LEMON DROP APPLE WOOD SMOKED WINGS

I'll eat my shorts if these aren't the best damn wings you've ever had. We're talking a maple syrup and lemon juice coating, then smoking the wings over apple wood. You can leave out the whisky (although it adds a pretty crazy taste dimension) if you're serving kids. It's very important to rinse and pat dry the wings to get the skin good and crispy. Yield: 20 whole wings

20 whole chicken wings ("drumette" and
   "wingette" attached), rinsed and patted dry

2 tablespoons peanut oil or vegetable oil
   (30 ml)

Salt and pepper to taste

Maple lemon sauce:

2 tablespoons (30 ml) lemon zest

1/2 cup (125 ml) lemon juice

1/3 cup (85 ml) pure maple syrup

2 tablespoons (60 ml) fresh grated ginger

3 tablespoons (45 ml) bourbon whisky

2 tablespoons (30 ml) fresh mint, chopped fine

Salt and pepper to taste

6 cups (1.5 L) apple wood chips, 4 cups
   (1 L) of the chips soaked in cool water
   for one hour and drained.

Splash of bourbon

- To make the maple lemon sauce, combine all ingredients in a small bowl and whisk. Reserve.

- To make the smoke pouches, see page 37. Use 2 cups (500 ml) of soaked chips and 1 cup (250 ml) of the dry. Mix the wood chips together, splash in some bourbon – about 2 tablespoons (30 ml).

- Rinse chicken and pat dry. Sprinkle liberally with salt and pepper and drizzle with oil.

- Prepare barbecue for indirect cooking and smoking: 220F (104C).

- Turn one side of the barbecue to low heat. Leave the other side off and slip a drip pan under the grates of the no heat side. Place the smoke pouch on direct heat. Wait for smoke, then reduce heat to 220F (104C), if necessary.

- Oil grill. Place wings on the grill over the drip pan.

- Close the lid and slow smoke for 1 1/2 hours, changing the smoke pouch when the smoke dissipates. Baste with maple lemon sauce in the last 1/2 hour.

- Remove from grill and toss all together with the leftover maple lemon sauce.

MESQUITE SMOKED CAPON

A capon is a young, castrated male rooster (and you thought chickens had it bad). It's larger than your average non-steroid chicken and has rich sweet meat. A nice grain-fed chicken will do if you can't find a capon, although your butcher will be mighty impressed when you ask for one. I know it looks like there are a lot of steps to this recipe, but really the BBQ does most of the work. Yield: 6–8 healthy portions

1 6-lb (2.7 kg) fresh capon

Marinade:

1/2 cup (125 ml) olive oil

1/4 cup (60 ml) fresh lemon juice

1/4 cup (60 ml) fresh orange juice

1/4 cup (60 ml) red wine vinegar

2–3 tablespoons (30-45 ml) Piri Piri,
   or another hot pepper sauce

2 teaspoons (10 ml) paprika

1/2 teaspoon (2.5 ml) ground cumin

2 tablespoons (30 ml) chopped fresh
   parsley, leaves only

2 teaspoons (10 ml) finely chopped
   fresh ginger

2 teaspoons (10 ml) chopped fresh thyme,
   stems removed

1 tablespoon (15 ml) chopped fresh garlic

- Rinse the capon and pat dry.

- Place the marinade ingredients in a medium sized bowl and whisk until combined. Reserve 1/2 cup (125 ml) for basting.

- Place the capon in a large sealable plastic bag. Pour the marinade over and marinate for 8–12 hours in the refrigerator.

- Prepare stuffing by melting the butter in a large skillet set over medium heat. Add the chopped onions and garlic and sauté until translucent. Add the peppers, corn and fresh thyme leaves. Cook, stirring frequently for 3 minutes or until fragrant. Remove from heat; season to taste with salt and pepper.

- Add the chopped corn bread and stir gently until all flavours are incorporated. Cool completely.

- Remove chicken from marinade and discard marinade.

- Season the chicken with salt inside the cavity and outside all over the skin. Stuff the cavity with the now cooled cornbread stuffing. Place a long-handled stainless steel spoon in the centre of the stuffing. This is done to ensure the stuffing is fully cooked by acting as a heat conductor.

- Truss the capon. See page 96.

- Make 2 smoke pouches. See page 37.

Stuffing:

2 tablespoons (30 ml) unsalted butter

2 teaspoons (10 ml) finely chopped garlic

1 cup (250 ml) fresh corn kernels or canned

1/2 cup (125 ml) medium diced yellow onion
    (1/4-inch/6-mm dice)

1/4 cup (60 ml) red pepper, chopped

2 cups (500 ml) day-old cornbread cut into
    1/2-inch (1.3cm) cubes

2 teaspoons (10 ml) fresh chopped thyme
    (stems removed)

1 teaspoon (5 ml) fresh ground black pepper

Salt to taste

6 cups (1.5 L) mesquite wood chips, 4 cups
    (1 L) soaked in cool water for one hour
    and drained

- Preheat barbecue for medium indirect cooking and smoking: 350F (176C). Turn one side of barbecue on high and leave other side off. Place a drip pan under grills of the no heat side.

- Place smoke pouch directly on burner. Close lid, wait for smoke. Once barbecue is smoking adjust heat. Place chicken on no heat side over drip pan.

- After 30 minutes change the smoke pouch and baste the chicken with reserved marinade.

- Chicken should take about 16 minutes per pound. (Approximately 30 minutes per kilogram)

- To test chicken, insert an instant read thermometer into the thickest part of the thigh (away from the bone). It should read 165F–170 (74–76 C).

- Remove from grill, cover with foil and let rest for 15 minutes.

- Once rested, scoop all stuffing from the cavity and carve the chicken.

POMEGRANATE MOLASSES TURKEY BREAST

You can actually buy pomegranate molasses in any Middle Eastern grocery store, but we've given you a quick recipe to make your own. Pomegranates are being marketed as a "superfruit" these days because they are apparently high in nutrients and anti-oxidants. Super or not, they're delicious and make a unique marinade for the turkey. Any good butcher will be pleased to sell you the turkey breast without having to buy the whole bird.

Yield: 6 servings

1 2-lb (900 g) boneless skinless turkey breast

Marinade:

1 cup (250 ml) pomegranate juice

2 tablespoons (30 ml) molasses

2 teaspoons (10 ml) finely chopped
     fresh garlic

1 medium red onion, finely diced

2 tablespoons (30 ml) fresh mint, roughly
     chopped

2 teaspoons (10 ml) brown sugar

1 teaspoon (5 ml) ground cardamom

2 tablespoons (30 ml) lemon zest

2 tablespoons (30 ml) fresh lemon juice

Salt and pepper to taste

- Combine marinade ingredients in a small saucepan set over medium heat. Bring the mixture to a gentle simmer while stirring. Reduce heat and simmer until liquid has thickened slightly, about 5 minutes. Remove from heat and cool completely.

- Place turkey breast in a large sealable plastic bag and pour three quarters of the marinade over the turkey. Reserve the remaining marinade for basting the turkey when grilling. Place the turkey in the refrigerator and marinate for 4 hours.

- Preheat barbecue to medium: 350F (175C). Oil grill.

- Remove turkey from marinade, place on the grill and cook for 12 minutes per side or until the juices run clear. Baste the turkey every 6 minutes.

- Remove from grill, cover loosely with foil and let rest for 15 minutes before slicing.

PROSCIUTTO WRAPPED CHICKEN BREAST STUFFED WITH GOAT CHEESE

This is an invite-the-boss-over-for-dinner type recipe. You can make these up in the morning, wrap them in plastic and stick them in the fridge. Just remember to take them out of the fridge 15 minutes before BBQing so they can return to room temperature. The combo of salty crisp prosciutto wrapped around an oregano-studded goat cheese-stuffed chicken breast is a taste and texture riot. For this you'll want a fruity dry white wine. Yield: 6 servings

6 organic free run chicken breasts, 7 oz
   (200 g) each

1 cup (250 ml) fresh goat cheese, crumbled

1 tablespoon (15 ml) fresh oregano leaves,
   loosely chopped

1 tablespoon (20 ml) plus 1 teaspoon
   maple syrup

1 tablespoon (15 ml) lemon zest

Cracked black pepper to taste

12 thin slices of prosciutto ham

Olive oil for brushing

- In a medium bowl mix together goat cheese, oregano, lemon zest, maple syrup and pepper.

- Make a horizontal cut in each chicken breast to create a pocket and stuff each pocket with mixture.

- Season outside of chicken with pepper. Wrap 2 pieces of prosciutto around breast and tightly wrap each breast in plastic wrap. Place into the refrigerator to set up for 20–30 minutes.

- Remove plastic wrap and drizzle each prosciutto-wrapped breast with olive oil.

- Preheat grill to medium indirect heat: 350F (176C). Leave one burner off.

- Oil the grates. Place the chicken on grill over the direct heat side.

- Grill chicken for about 2–3 minutes, turning and moving the breasts around the grill so the prosciutto cooks evenly without getting too charred, rather golden and crispy.

- Once that is accomplished move chicken to the indirect heat side. Close the lid and continue to cook for 10–12 minutes or until the juices from the chicken run clear when poked.

- Remove from grill and let rest for 5 minutes. Don't tent with foil or that nice prosciutto crust will go soggy.

- Slice into 1/2-inch (1.2 cm) portions.

PULL THE RIP CORD JERK WINGS

Can you tell we like Jamaican jerk seasoning? We use this spice combo a few times throughout the book because it's such a versatile rub. Serve these wings with some good quality salty potato chips and sliced raw carrots for lunch. Yield: 20 whole wings

20 whole chicken wings ("drumette" and "wingette" attached) rinsed and patted dry

Rub:

2 tablespoons (30 ml) ground coriander

2 tablespoons (30 ml) ground ginger

2 tablespoons (30 ml) lightly packed brown sugar

1 tablespoon (15 ml) onion powder

1 tablespoon (15 ml) garlic powder

1 tablespoon (15 ml) salt

2 teaspoons (10 ml) ground habanero or cayenne pepper

2 teaspoons (10 ml) ground black pepper

2 teaspoons dried thyme leaves (10 ml)

1 teaspoon ground cinnamon (5 ml)

1 teaspoon ground allspice (5 ml)

1/2 tsp ground cloves (2.5 ml)

Vegetable oil for brushing

Fresh cilantro and sliced lime for garnish

- Combine all ingredients for the rub in a bowl and mix.

- Rinse and pat dry the wings. Massage the rub into the wings, all over and quite aggressively as to tear little micro pockets of flavour into the flesh. Place in the refrigerator for 2–4 hours to marinate.

- Preheat grill to medium: 350F (176C). Oil grill.

- Place wings on grill and cook for approximately 10 minutes or until caramelized and golden brown on one side.

- Flip and continue to cook a further 10–15 minutes or until fully cooked and golden brown.

- Remove from grill.

TEA SMOKED DUCK WITH LIME HOISIN SAUCE

Here's a killer BBQ recipe with an amazing Asian influence. We take a few liberties to make this dish different from any Chinese duck your guests have ever had. First we add tart lime juice to the hoisin sauce for a kick they're not expecting. Then we smoke the duck using rice and tea instead of wood chips. Pretty cool, huh? Yield: 6 servings

4 whole boneless duck breasts, skin on

Rub:

1/2 cup (125 ml) dark brown sugar

1/4 cup (60 ml) Chinese 5-spice

Pepper to taste

Hoisin lime sauce:

1/2 cup (125 ml) grape seed oil

2 tablespoons (30 ml) minced garlic

1 tablespoon (15 ml) minced fresh ginger

2 cups (500 ml) hoisin sauce

1/2 cup (125 ml) fresh lime juice

Smoke tray:

2 cups (500 ml) rice

1 cup (250 ml) green tea leaves

- Combine rub ingredients in a small bowl.

- With a sharp knife, make slashes in a crisscross pattern through the fat of the duck breast to aid in rendering the fat and to allow the rub flavour to get in. Ensure you don't cut into the flesh.

- Rub the duck all over with rub ingredients, place in a plastic bag and marinate overnight.

- Remove from marinade. Discard excess.

- To make the hoisin sauce, mix all ingredients together just to combine.

- Prepare smoke tray by mixing the tea with the rice. Place in a disposable aluminum container to fit your barbecue burner.

- Preheat barbecue to 220F (104C) for low smoking. Leave one burner on and 2 off. Place the rice/tea mixture over direct heat in the aluminum container. Place a drip pan under the side without heat.

- Place duck breasts over the drip pan and smoke for 30 minutes for medium rare. Baste the duck with half of the hoisin lime sauce 2–3 times while cooking. Reserve the rest for dipping.

- Remove from barbecue, tent loosely with foil and let rest 15 minutes.

- Slice thin and serve with hoisin lime sauce.

TURKEY PASTRAMI

Yes, you read right: turkey pastrami. What makes pastrami pastrami is the way the meat is prepared and we do to turkey what your favourite deli does to a beef brisket but we do it with a *Road Grill* BBQ twist. Excellent on sandwiches of course and keeps in the fridge for a week so you can go back for multiple late night snacks. Yield: 15 sandwiches

1 5-lb (2.26 kg) turkey breast, bone in
*   (rib bones removed) and skin on*

Rub:

3 tablespoons (45 ml) coriander seeds,
*   crushed*

3 tablespoons (45 ml) cracked pepper

1 1/2 tablespoons (22.5 ml) chopped garlic

1 tablespoon (15 ml) yellow mustard seeds

1/4 cup (60 ml) course salt

1/4 cup (60 ml) brown sugar

2 tablespoons (30 ml) Spanish paprika

2 tablespoons (30 ml) fresh minced ginger

6 cups (1.5 L) hickory wood chips, 4 cups
*   (1 L) of the chips soaked in cool water*
*   for 1 hour and drained*
Rye bread or crusty rolls
Variety of mustards and pickles

- Place the coriander seeds in a dishtowel and crush them with a heavy skillet. Combine the cracked seeds with remaining rub ingredients in a small bowl and mix.

- Rub the mixture all over the turkey quite aggressively to tear little micro pockets of flavour into the meat. Place in a large sealable plastic baggie and allow curing overnight in the refrigerator. (You will have to turn the bag 2 or 3 times.)

- Make 2 smoke pouches (see page 37).

- Remove turkey from the baggie and place on tray. Discard excess marinade (you will see all the moisture the cure has drawn from the breast). Pat dry.

- Prepare barbecue for indirect low heat and smoking. Turn one side of the grill to low heat: 220F (104C) and leave other side off. Place a drip pan under the no heat side of the barbecue. Oil grill.

- Place smoke pouch over the direct heat side. Place turkey on no heat side and close lid. Monitor the temperature to ensure it is 220F (104C).

- Slow smoke the turkey for 3 hours or until juices run clear. (Please note this time can vary pending on the turkey's density). Replace the smoke pouch when necessary.

- Test the turkey temperature with a meat thermometer. Temperature should read 165F (75C).

- Remove from barbecue, cover loosely with foil and let rest for 30 minutes.

- Cut the turkey thin and serve with lots of crusty rolls or rye bread and bowls of fun, funky mustards and pickles. This pastrami is great served hot or cold.

THAI GRILLED CHICKEN BURGER WITH MANGO SALSA

Coriander, turmeric and cumin make for a powerful flavour combo in this Asian influenced marinade for the chicken. Asian fish sauce is made from fermented fish and is widely available these days. It adds a depth of flavour to the dish along with that salty component. Yield: 6 Servings

6 boneless skinless chicken breasts

Marinade:

2 lemon grass stalks

3 fresh green chili peppers, seeded and chopped

3 green onions, chopped

1/2 teaspoon (2.5 ml) cumin

1/2 teaspoon (2.5 ml) ground turmeric

1 teaspoon (5 ml) ground coriander

Zest of one lime

3 tablespoons (45 ml) fresh lime juice

2 teaspoons (10 ml) grated fresh ginger

1 tablespoon (15 ml) fish sauce

2 teaspoons sugar (10 ml)

Spicy Mango Salsa
(see recipe page 250)

6 mini crusty baguette or rolls

2 cups (500 ml) mesclun greens

Vegetable oil for brushing

- Remove and discard the tough outer skin from the lemon grass stalks and roughly chop. Toss it and all the marinade ingredients into a food processor; process until smooth.

- Place the chicken in a large plastic sealable baggie. Pour the marinade over and toss the baggie to ensure chicken in evenly coated. Marinate in the refrigerator for 1 hour.

- Preheat barbecue to medium high: 375F (190C). Oil grill.

- Remove chicken from the marinade, drizzle with oil and season with salt and pepper. Place chicken on the grill and cook 3–4 minutes per side with barbecue lid up.

- Chicken is cooked when the flesh is opaque and the juices run clear.

- Serve on a toasted baguette with greens and Spicy Mango Salsa.

Fish and Shellfish

It's odd that we always lump fish and shellfish together in one category, that being "seafood," just because they both come from the water. A cow and a chicken have more in common than an oyster and a halibut but you'd never see beef and poultry in the same chapter.

In broad general terms "fish" is all the stuff that swims and "shellfish" is all the stuff that doesn't but has a shell. The phrase has always struck me as odd (do we say, "think I'll have some *landfood* for dinner tonight"?). It was probably dreamed up by some advertising wonk trying to increase sales.

A lot of people are less comfortable at the BBQ with fish and shellfish than they are with landfood (if I write it enough maybe people will start saying it). Thing is, seafood is actually way easier to cook. It's done faster and doesn't take as long to marinate. But fish can dry out quickly and fall apart on the grill and nobody wants to sit down to a plateful of dried out fish chunks. That's why North Americans consume twice as much fish in restaurants as they do at home. You like fish, you'd just prefer someone else do the cooking. Well, read on and let's see if we can change that.

The 3 most important things to know when buying fish:

FIND A FISHMONGER First of all, *where* you buy your fish is very important. Find a fishmonger and make him your friend. Do not buy fish in a giant grocery store. A store that sells fish and only fish will have staff who actually know something about the product they're selling. They can give you advice, answer your questions and tell you where the fish is from and how long it's been out of the water.

FISH FILLETS SHOULD SMELL LIKE THE SEA Fish fillets or steaks should never be displayed on ice. They should always be in refrigerated display counters with a glass front. Ask the guy behind the counter to pull out specific fillets or steaks to show you (he should be wearing hygienic gloves, by the way). Now take a whiff. If it smells fishy, it's an old bit of fish and they have no business selling it. The fish should have a faint scent of the sea (some say almost like cucumber). Also, look for nicks or dark splotches, which give you a hint that the fish had a rough life. Some people suggest you do the touch test to see if the fish is nice and firm. I would suggest you stop shopping at a store that lets complete strangers poke at exposed fish flesh. Smell is the way to go.

GIVE WHOLE FISH THE ONCE-OVER Whole fish can be displayed on ice. Once again, the scent should be faint and not fishy. Check out the eyes. They should be clear; not milky or clouded over. Pull the gills back and see if they're bright red inside (black is no good). Feel the skin. If it's clammy or sticky then move on.

The 3 most important things to know when grilling fish and seafood:

DON'T OVER-MARINATE All eating fish have delicate flesh. There is no such thing as a "tough cut" of fish that needs lots of marinating like you'd get with landfood (it's growing on you, isn't it?). That's because fish do not have the tough connective tissues, muscles and tendons to toughen it up. Some fish are fattier and some have more bones, but all fish is delicate and should not be subjected to extended marinating. This is particularly true if your marinade has an acidic component like lemon juice, wine or vinegar because it "cooks" the fish (like seviche) and can render it tough and chewy (same goes for shellfish like shrimp or scallops). Follow the recipe directions closely and note the amount of time required for marinating. While we always encourage you to mess with ingredients, don't mess with the time.

OIL THE HOT GRILL *AND* THE FISH The single biggest complaint people have about barbecuing fish is that it sticks to the grill. Here's how you make sure that doesn't happen. Get the grill nice and hot and oil it just before you grill the fish. Make sure you wipe the fish dry with paper towel and then oil the fish. You wipe the fish dry because any condensation will steam when it hits the hot grill rather than produce the nice char marks.

WATCH THE CLOCK AND LEAVE THE FISH ALONE Once you've got the fish on the grill, leave it alone. If the recipe says wait 5 minutes before turning, then wait 5 minutes. Do not peek to see if there are char marks. The fish isn't ready to be turned and will stick to the grill and fall apart. Also, if the recipe says 5 minutes per side then cook it for 5 minutes a side and *not a second longer*. An extra minute a side might seem like nothing but that's an increase of 20% in cooking time and that's how you end up with dry fish that falls apart on you. If anything, err on the side of caution and do 4 minutes and change per side because the fish will continue to cook once it's off the grill.

The 3 things you need to know about buying shellfish:

1 SHRIMP Do not *ever* buy farmed shrimp. There are lots of good arguments for and against farmed fish, but there is absolutely no reason to buy farmed shrimp. Those black razorback things? Walk away. Farmed shrimp are tasteless and mainly come from Asia where they do not have the health and safety regulations we do over here. Farmed shrimp are raised in stagnant putrid water. They suck, they are no good. Do not buy them. Subtle, aren't I? (However, farmed mussels are excellent and a lot of oysters are moved to specific beds before harvesting and they're all great.)

2 LOBSTER Female lobsters make the best eats, plus you get the roe and the tomalley. Ask your fishmonger to pick out the females for you. You can tell a lobster is female if it is wider at the tail (that would be the hips). If you flip a lobster over on its back, the last little pair of wiggly leg thingies on a boy are firm and erect; they're soft and pliable on a girl. Hey, I don't make this stuff up.

3 SCALLOPS whenever possible buy "dry" scallops. When a scallop is harvested, the guys in the boat shuck them on the spot. On some boats the scallops are immediately frozen (this is "dry"). Others put them in a water bath treated with chemicals that "plump up" the scallop thereby increasing its weight and value on the scales. This would be a "wet" scallop and they're the ones that ooze that slimy milky liquid when you cook them.

What about tenting with tinfoil?
Do I have to do this with fish, too?

Good news, fish doesn't have any of that connective tissue and stuff to
tighten up while cooking. It therefore doesn't need to "relax" for a bit once
it comes off the grill. Told you cooking fish was easy.

BBQ'D SHRIMP PIZZA ON A RED PEPPER PESTO CRUST

This is what you call gourmet pizza. The "21/25" count refers to how many shrimp you'll roughly get to the pound. You can buy frozen pizza dough at most supermarkets or see whether a local pizzeria will sell you some (hey, it's worth asking). Make an extra big batch of the red pepper pesto to use as a sauce with pasta or a spread on sandwiches. Yield: 1 large pizza, 6–8 slices

Pizza:

1 lb (454 g) pre-made pizza dough

12 large peeled and deveined fresh
    shrimp (21/25 count)

2 teaspoons (10 ml) fresh garlic, chopped fine

1 cup (250 ml) fresh goat cheese, crumbled

1/2 cup (125 ml) thinly sliced red onion

1/4 cup (60 ml) black olives, pitted and halved

1/2 cup (125 ml) cooked (crispy) pancetta
    bacon, roughly chopped

1/4 cup (60 ml) fresh chopped parsley

All purpose flour for dusting

Pesto:

1 large red bell pepper

1 clove garlic, minced fine

2 tablespoons (30 ml) olive oil

1/2 teaspoon (2.5 ml) balsamic vinegar

1/2 cup (125 ml) grated Parmesan cheese

1/4 cup (60 ml) fresh basil leaves,
    roughly chopped

Salt and pepper to taste

- Place the shrimp in a sealable plastic bag with the olive oil and minced garlic. Toss to evenly coat and marinate in the refrigerator for 1 hour.

- Preheat barbecue to high heat: 450F–475.

- Remove shrimp from marinade and season with salt and pepper. Lightly brush the pepper with oil.

- Oil barbecue grill. Place the shrimps and the pepper on the grill.

- Cook the shrimp for approximately 1 minute per side or until the shrimp has golden char marks and has just begun to turn pink.

- Remove from grill and set aside

- Grill the pepper directly on grill, turning often until the skin is blackened all over. Remove the pepper and place in a paper bag. (This will encourage the skin to come off easily).

- Peel the pepper and remove the seeds and core. Place the pepper into a food processor with the garlic and puree until smooth. With the processor running, gradually add the olive oil and vinegar.

- Stir in the cheese, basil and season with salt and pepper.

- Preheat barbecue to high: 450F–475F (230C–245C) on one side and leave the other side without heat. Place a pizza stone on the side without heat and preheat for 15 minutes. Oil barbecue grills.

- Roll the pizza dough out on a lightly floured surface into a 14-inch (36 cm) circle.

- Place the dough onto a generously floured pizza peel or cutting board.

- Spread the pesto on the crust evenly. Top with red onion, goat cheese, black olives and bacon.

- Slide the pizza on the preheated pizza stone. Close the lid and cook for 10–12 minutes or until the crust is golden brown and has bubbled up.

- Meanwhile, slice the shrimp in half lengthwise.

- Slide the pizza over to the direct heat side. Sprinkle the shrimp equally over the pizza.

- Cook with the lid down for 2–3 more minutes until you have a slight char on the bottom of the crust.

- Remove from grill, cool slightly and cut into portions. Sprinkle with fresh parsley.

BLACKENED SCALLOPS WITH AVOCADO CORN RELISH

Normally I'm not a big fan of blackened spice mixes but it really works here. We've turned the heat down a bit in the recipe so you can still taste the scallop. Ask your fishmonger for "dry" scallops which means they haven't been soaking in water. Soaking plumps them up which means they'll leave that milky white ooze when you cook them. These are perfect appetizers for a grown-up pool party. Yield: 24 appetizer portions

12 large scallops

1 1/2 tablespoons (22.5 ml) blackening spice
   (recipe follows)

2 cups (500 ml) avocado corn salsa (see below)

24 large tortilla chips

Blackening spice:

1 tablespoon (15 ml) paprika

1 teaspoon (5 ml) dried thyme leaves

1 teaspoon (5 ml) ground cayenne

1/2 teaspoon (2.5 ml) white pepper

1 teaspoon (5 ml) garlic powder

1 teaspoon (5 ml) onion powder

Avocado corn salsa:

2 ripe avocados, peeled, pitted and
   coarsely mashed

2 tablespoons (30 ml) finely chopped red onion

2 tablespoons (30 ml) finely sliced green onion

1 cup (250 ml) roasted corn kernels
   (see page 200)

1/4 cup (60 ml) roughly chopped
   fresh cilantro leaves

Juice of 1 large lime

1/2 teaspoon (2.5 ml) ground cumin

1/2 teaspoon (2.5 ml) chili powder

Salt and pepper to taste

- To make corn salsa, mash the avocado roughly with a fork in a medium bowl. Add the remaining ingredients and mix well.

- To make the blackening spice, place all ingredients in a bowl and mix to combine evenly.

- Rinse scallops, pat dry and sprinkle evenly on both sides with the blackening spice.

- Preheat grill to high: 475F–500F (246C–260C). Oil grill.

- Place scallops directly on the well-oiled grill. Cook without moving them for approximately 1 1/2 minutes per side.

- Remove scallops from grill, slice in half through the circumference.

- Place a dollop of avocado salsa on a chip and top with blackened scallop. Repeat with remaining scallops and serve.

BLACK BEAN MUSSELS

Most people don't think mussels when they think BBQ. Yes, you do them in a big pot just like you would on the stove and no they don't get grilled or smoked or anything. But hey, it's summertime. It's hot and sticky. Do you really want to be stuck in the kitchen? Your trusty BBQ doubles as a cook top for non-traditional BBQ fare, like mussels. This recipe has a black bean Asian twist to it. Serve the mussels hot with crusty bread and maybe some sweet grilled corn (see page 200). Yield: 6 appetizer servings

2 lb (907 g) mussels, cleaned and bearded

1 tablespoon (15 ml) minced garlic

1/4 cup (60 ml) green onion, sliced thin
  (reserve some for garnish)

1/4 cup (60 ml) red onion, diced

1 yellow pepper, sliced thin

1 red pepper, sliced thin (reserve some
  for garnish)

1 tablespoon (15 ml) chopped fresh ginger

1 tablespoon (15 ml) store-bought
  black beans in hoisin sauce

3/4 cup (180 ml) dry white wine

1/2 cup (125 ml) 35% whipping cream

Pepper

- Place all ingredients in bowl and using tongs mix well.

- Preheat barbecue for super high cooking: 500F–660F (260C–315C), or as high as your barbecue goes.

- Place a large, covered cast iron pot on the grill, close barbecue lid and preheat about 10 minutes.

- Using barbecue gloves, lift the lid of the pot and carefully pour the mussel mixture into the hot pot. Stir, cover, and close barbecue lid.

- Cook mussels for about 4–5 minutes or until they just start to open.

- Using gloves, remove pot from grill.

- Ladle mussels with sauce into bowls, discarding any unopened mussels.

- Garnish with cilantro and thin sliced peppers.

CITRUS TEA RUBBED HALIBUT WITH ORZO FENNEL ORANGE SALAD

No freaking out because the recipe calls for dried fruit zest. Zests are available at most Chinese grocery stores, but they are also easy to make. Zest the fruits and spread on a baking sheet, bake at 200F (93C) until the zests are dried, about 2 hours. Serves 6

6 6-oz (170 g) fresh halibut fillets,
  skin removed

2 tablespoons (30 ml) grape seed or
  canola oil

Salad:

2 cups (500 ml) cooked orzo pasta

2 oranges, segmented

Juice of 1 orange

Juice of 1 lemon

2 medium fennel bulbs, stalks removed, halved
  vertically, cored and sliced 1/8-inch thick

1 tablespoon (15 ml) olive oil, plus more
  for garnish

Kosher salt and freshly ground pepper

Tea Rub:

2 tablespoons (30 ml) green tea leaves

1 tablespoon (15 ml) dried peppermint leaves

2 tablespoons (30 ml) lemongrass flakes

1 teaspoon (5 ml) kosher salt

1 teaspoon (5 ml) turbinado or brown sugar

1 tablespoon (15 ml) dried orange zest, crushed

1 tablespoon (15 ml) dried lime zest

2 teaspoons (10 ml) dried lemon zest

1 1/2 teaspoons (7.5 g) ground ginger

- To make the salad, combine the orzo, orange segments and juice, lemon juice, fennel, and olive oil in a medium bowl. Toss to evenly combine and season with salt and pepper.

- To make the rub, combine all ingredients in a small bowl and mix to combine.

- Place the rub on a large plate and press both sides of the halibut into it. Drizzle with the grape seed oil.

- Preheat barbecue to moderate-high: 425F (220C). Oil grill.

- Place the fish on the grill and grill for 3–4 minutes per side or until desired doneness.

- Remove from grill and serve with fennel salad. Drizzle each plate with olive oil.

CRAB STUFFED AVOCADOS

Creamy avocado topped with sweet crabmeat. Yum. Remember to pick through the crabmeat for little bits of shell. It doesn't happen often but a shell isn't really something you want to bite into. By the way, the word "avocado" is derived from the Aztec word for testicle. I leave it up to you to figure out why. You'll note there's no barbecuing involved – one of those recipes for scorching summer days when it's too hot even to BBQ. Serves 6

3 ripe Hass avocados

2 limes, juiced

1 1/2 tablespoons (22.5 ml) hot sauce

1/2 cup (125 ml) mayonnaise

3 tablespoons (45 ml) fresh chopped chives

2 teaspoons (10 ml) honey

1 1/2 pounds (680 g) lump crabmeat

Salt and pepper to taste

1 bunch watercress, rinsed and dried

3 limes, halved

- Halve the avocados, remove the pit and using a large spoon, separate the flesh from the skin, keeping the halves as intact as possible.

- Coat the halves all over with lime juice to prevent discolouration. Season the flesh with salt and pepper.

- In a medium bowl combine the hot sauce, mayonnaise, chives, honey and crabmeat. Mix until well combined and season with salt and pepper.

- Fill the avocado halves with the crab mixture. Serve on a bed of watercress with a half a lime squeezed over the greens and avocado.

CURED AND SMOKED SALMON

This is absolutely the best smoked salmon I've ever had. Curing the salmon in whisky, then brown sugar, maple syrup and all the other stuff "candies" the salmon flesh giving it a crazy texture. Seriously, do this recipe. You're going to love it. Make sure your fishmonger removes all the pin bones. Yield: 1 whole salmon fillet

1 whole salmon fillet, about 2 lb (907 g),
    skin on and pin bones removed
1 cup (250 ml) whisky

Maple syrup cure:
1/2 cup (125 ml) brown sugar
1/2 cup (125 ml) maple syrup
1 tablespoon (15 ml) fresh ginger,
    chopped fine
1/2 cup (125 ml) course kosher salt
1 teaspoon (5 ml) dried chili flakes
Zest of one lemon
2 sprigs fresh thyme
1 tablespoon (15 ml) cracked black pepper

3 cups (750 ml) alder wood or apple wood
    chips; 2 cups (500 ml) of the chips soaked
    in cold water for 1 hour and drained).
Splash of whisky for the smoke pouch

- Place the salmon in a large flat container, pour the whisky over and marinate at room temperature for 20 minutes. Drain and pat dry.

- To make the cure, combine all ingredients in a medium bowl. Spread 1/2 of the cure on the bottom of a square pan. Place the salmon flesh-side down onto the cure. Place the rest of the cure on top of the skin and rub the sides as well.

- Place a foil-covered heavy object onto salmon to weight it down. Refrigerate for 8 hours and up to overnight.

- Rinse salmon with cold water and pat dry. You should notice a colour change and the flesh should be firm as the cure actually cooks the salmon.

- Prepare smoke pouch (see page 37). Use 2 cups (500 ml) of the soaked chips with 1 cup (250 ml) of the dry and add a splash of whisky.

- Prepare barbecue for indirect smoking: 220F (104C). Leave one burner with the grate removed on high and the other off. Place smoke pouch on the burner that's on high and wait for smoke.

- Oil the grill. Place salmon skin-side down on grill on the no heat side and smoke for 10–15 minutes. The salmon has already cooked by the cure marinade – it just needs a little smoke flavour without changing its texture.

- Place in the refrigerator for 1–2 hours to firm up.

- Slice thin using a very sharp fillet knife. Serve with mini bagels or crusty bread, cream cheese, onions and capers.

FRESH GRILLED TROUT WITH ROASTED PEACHES

Trout is one of those catch-all names used in the fish world (like bass and sardine) and refers to a number of different freshwater fish in the salmon family. Trout has a mild sweet flavour and medium-firm flesh that holds up nicely on the grill (skin on, please). In this recipe we pair trout with grilled peaches mixed into a sage chutney – delicious and very simple to make. The chutney also goes well with grilled pork tenderloin by the way. Serves 6

6 7-oz (170–200 g) steelhead trout fillets,
   skin on, scaled and pin bones removed
2 tablespoons (30 ml) olive oil
Salt and pepper to taste
2 lemons
Olive oil for brushing

Roasted peaches with sage chutney:
6 freestone peaches, cut in half and
   pit removed
1 small red onion
1 tablespoon (15 ml) fresh sage, stems
   removed and thinly sliced
Juice of 1 large navel orange
Splash of sherry vinegar
Salt and pepper to taste

- Prepare the peaches for the grill – place them in a bowl and drizzle with olive oil and season with salt and pepper.

- Cut the onion into 1/2-inch wedges being sure to keep the root of the onion intact as it will hold together well on the barbecue. Drizzle the onion with olive oil and season with salt and pepper.

- Brush both sides of the trout with olive oil and season with salt and pepper.

- Prepare barbecue for direct medium-high heat grilling: 375F (190C). Oil grill.

- Place the fish flesh-side down directly on grill and sprinkle salt on the skin side. Cook for 2 minutes or until nice char marks are achieved. Flip fish and continue to cook for a further 2–3 minutes. Remove from grill. The fish is hot and will continue to cook slightly.

- Grill the peaches on the same grill and at the same temperature as the fish. (This can and should all be done at the same time) Place peaches flesh-side down and cook for 2–3 minutes until caramelized. Flip and continue to cook skin side for 2 minutes.

- Grill onions on each side 2–4 minutes until they are softened and nice golden char marks are achieved.

- Remove peaches and onions from the grill. Slip the skins off the peaches (they should slide off easily), place in a bowl and using a fork, mash the peaches slightly. Petal off the onions from the root (discard root), mix into the peaches and add the sage, sherry vinegar, and orange juice. Season with salt and pepper. Serve each fillet with a dollop of chutney.

GRILLED CLAMS IN THE SHELL WITH SERRANO HAM

As with most things, size does matter when it comes to clams, only here's a case where smaller is better – the bigger the clam, the chewier. Little necks are the perfect size and have a clean sweet taste when grilled in the shell and served with spicy Serrano ham. This also makes a great topping for linguine, with olive oil, roasted garlic and freshly grated Parmesan Reggiano.

Yield: 30 little neck clams

30 little neck fresh clams, scrubbed

10 slices of Serrano ham, cut into
    bite-sized pieces

Dressing:

Juice of 2 lemons

1 teaspoon (5 ml) hot sauce or more to taste

1 teaspoon (5 ml) Dijon mustard

2 tablespoons (45 ml) finely chopped
    flat leaf parsley

1/4 cup (60 ml) extra virgin olive oil

Pepper to taste

- Preheat barbecue to high: 475F–500F (245C-260C) and oil grill.

- To make the dressing, place all ingredients in a small Mason jar with a lid. Shake vigorously until well combined.

- Place the clams directly on the grate of the grill, close the cover, and cook until clams open, about 5 minutes (discard any clams that do not open).

- Remove from grill, place a piece of ham into each clam and drizzle with a little dressing.

- Serve hot.

HALIBUT WITH CURRIED CORN SAUCE

How cool is this? A halibut starts out as a round fish with an eye on each side of its head. But, after about 6 months, one eye moves over to the other side of its head and it becomes a flat fish. (And you thought all you were getting when you bought this book was great BBQ recipes.) While we always encourage you to mess with the recipes, in this case don't go crazy with the curry as you don't want to bury the tastes of the apple and corn. Serves 6

6 7-oz (200g) halibut fillets, skin removed

3 tablespoons (45 ml) olive oil

Salt and pepper to taste

Corn sauce:

2 tablespoons (30 ml) unsalted butter

1/2 cup (125 ml) medium diced Spanish onion

1 teaspoon (5 ml) finely chopped garlic

1 1/2 teaspoons (23 ml) grated fresh ginger

1/2 medium green apple peeled, cored
    and diced

1 1/2 tablespoons (22.5 ml) madras curry paste

1/2 cup (125 ml) low sodium chicken stock

1 1/2 cups (375 ml) coconut milk

1 cup (250 ml) fresh corn kernels

1/4 cup (60 ml) fresh cilantro leaves,
    roughly chopped, for garnish

- In a medium saucepan set over medium heat, bring the coconut milk to a boil. Reduce heat to low, add the curry paste and simmer for 10 minutes.

- Melt butter in a large sauté pan set over medium heat. Add the onions, garlic, ginger and apple. Cook while stirring until onion is translucent and fragrant.

- Deglaze the pan with the chicken stock and cook a further 1–2 minutes until reduced by half. Add the coconut curry mixture, reduce heat to low and simmer for 3–4 minutes. Add the corn to the sauce and cook just to warm the kernels, about 1 minute.

- Preheat barbecue to medium high: 475F (245C). Oil grill.

- Drizzle the halibut with oil on both sides and season with salt and pepper.

- Place fish on the grill and cook without moving it for about 2–3 minutes per side or until the fish has deep golden char marks.

- Remove fish from grill, serve with warm sauce and sprinkle liberally with fresh cilantro.

GRILLED LOBSTER WITH GRAPEFRUIT SALSA

A lot of people are squeamish about dispatching a lobster. These days we've become so disconnected from our food – we don't know where it comes from or how it got on our plate. So it's a good idea to try recipes like this one every so often. Please note we've added the step of parboiling the lobster before BBQing. Don't cook the lobster for any longer than 2 minutes or they'll be tough and chewy. Serves 6

6 live lobsters, 1 1/2 lb (680 g) each

2 tablespoons olive oil (30 ml)

Juice of 2 lemons

Salsa:

2 medium sized pink grapefruit

1/4 cup (60 ml) olive oil

3 tablespoons (45 ml) fine chopped red onion

1 tablespoon (15 ml) green onion sliced thin

1/2 cup (125 ml) finely chopped red
    bell pepper

2 tablespoons (30 ml) cilantro leaves,
    roughly chopped

2 tablespoons (30 ml) fresh mint leaves,
    roughly chopped

1 tablespoon (15 ml) honey

1 tablespoon (15 ml) sherry wine vinegar

1 teaspoon (5 ml) lime zest

3 tablespoons (45 ml) fresh lime juice

Pinch of cayenne pepper

Kosher salt and freshly ground pepper
    to taste

6 bamboo skewers, soaked in cool water
    for 30 minutes

- For the salsa, slice off both ends of the grapefruit just enough to expose the flesh. Stand each grapefruit on a cutting board and, using a paring knife, cut away the peel and white pith from top to bottom in even strips, following curve of the grapefruit. Working over a bowl to catch the juices, slice between the membranes to release the segments.

- Place segments with juice in a small bowl. Add the remaining salsa ingredients and mix to combine the flavours.

- Preheat barbecue to high heat: 475F–500F (245C–260C). Oil grill.

- Place lobsters head first into a large pot of boiling salted water for just 2 minutes. Remove and cool slightly. Pull off the lobster tails, crack the shells or cut them open with a knife. Remove each tail in one piece.

- Run the soaked bamboo skewers through the tail lengthwise to keep it flat.

- Pull off the claws, crack and leave the meat inside. This will make it easier to pull the meat out.

- Brush meat with olive oil and season with salt and pepper. Place on preheated grill and cook for 2 minutes per side or until the meat is just cooked. Just before you remove the lobster, drizzle the meat with lemon juice.

- Serve with salsa.

GRILLED SNAPPER WITH ALMOND BROWN BUTTER

Brown butter is a classic sauce that's so simple to make. I promise this will become part of your regular weekday dinner rotation. As always, be careful not to overcook the fillets or you'll end up with a mouthful of dry. Serves 6

6 red snapper fillets, 5 oz (140 g each),
   scaled and de-boned
2 tablespoons (30 ml) olive oil
Sea salt and freshly ground pepper
   to taste
Lemon wedges for garnish

Sauce:
1/2 cup (125 ml) butter
1/2 cup (125 ml) sliced almonds
1 tablespoon (15 ml) orange zest

- Rub the fillets with oil and let stand 10 minutes. Sprinkle evenly with salt and pepper.

- Preheat barbecue to high: 500F (260C). Oil grill.

- Place fillet flesh-side down on the grill and cook for 2 minutes or until flesh is golden brown and releases easily from the grill. Flip and continue to cook a further 2 minutes. Remove from grill.

- Melt butter in a saucepan over medium-high heat; add the almonds and sauté for 5 minutes or until butter is golden brown. Remove from heat and stir in the zest.

- Spoon sauce evenly over grilled fish.

GRILLED SWORDFISH WITH CARIBBEAN SALSA

Swordfish is perfect on the BBQ because it's meaty and holds up well on the grill. The thing I love the most about quality fish (or any quality ingredient for that matter) is the fact that you really don't have to do much to it: a little oil, some salt and pepper and that's it. Let the BBQ do the work. We've "kabobed" the fish and matched it up with a spicy fruity Caribbean salsa. The salsa works really well with the sweet potato fries on page 182.

Serves 6–8

2 lb (907 g) swordfish, cut into 1 inch cubes

1–2 tablespoons (15–30 ml) vegetable oil or
   any neutral flavoured oil

Sea salt to taste

Good turn of fresh pepper

Caribbean salsa:

2 mangos, peeled, pitted and cut into
   1/4-inch (6 mm) dice

1/2 pineapple, peeled, cored and cut into
   1/4-inch dice

3 tablespoons (45 ml) red onion small dice

2 green onions, sliced thin

3 tablespoons (45 ml) fresh cilantro leaves,
   chopped roughly

1/2 Thai red chili, chopped fine

Juice of 2 limes

Juice and zest of 1 orange

Salt and pepper

10 bamboo skewers soaked in cool water
   for 30 minutes

Oil for brushing

Tin foil

- To make the salsa combine all the salsa ingredients in a medium bowl and mix. Taste and season with salt and pepper.

- Skewer the fish onto the soaked bamboo skewer, about 2–3 pieces per stick. Lightly brush the fish with oil and season with sea salt and fresh pepper.

- Prepare barbecue for direct medium- to high-heat grilling: 375F–425F (190C-218C). Oil the grill.

- Place the skewers directly on the grill and put a small sheet of foil under the exposed skewer to protect against burning.

- Grill for 1–2 minutes or until nice char marks are achieved. Flip and continue to cook until all sides are golden brown.

- Remove from grill and serve warm with the Caribbean salsa.

HABANERO MANGO GRILLED SHRIMP

This recipe calls for "21/25 count" shrimp. That's fishmonger talk for about how many you'd get in a pound. Get them peeled and deveined to cut down on prep time. Habanero chilies have more heat than jalapenos and are a bit sweeter. Remember: don't leave the shrimp in the marinade for more than an hour. If you do, the acidity of the lime and vinegar will "cook" them (that's how they make seviche) and they'll be rubbery when you pull them off the grill. Yield: 10 skewers

1 lb (454 g) fresh shrimp, 21/25 count, peeled and deveined (approximately 20 whole tail-on shrimp)

Sauce and marinade:

3 mangos, peeled, stone removed and roughly chopped

2 habanero chilies, seeded and chopped

2 green onions, roughly chopped

1 clove garlic, chopped fine

1 tablespoon (15 ml) finely chopped fresh ginger

1/4 cup (60 ml) roughly chopped cilantro leaves

1 cup (250 ml) rice wine vinegar

Juice of 2 limes

Salt to taste

20 skewers soaked in cool water for 30 minutes

Olive oil for brushing

- Place habanero, green onion, garlic, ginger and mango in a blender. Blend until smooth. Turn motor off and add cilantro and rice wine vinegar. Blend using on/off turns until evenly combined. Add salt if desired to taste.

- Place the shrimp in a sealable plastic baggie. Reserve 1 cup (250 ml) of marinade for basting and dipping. Pour the remaining marinade over shrimp and toss to coat. Marinate in the refrigerator for 1 hour.

- Remove shrimp from marinade and thread onto soaked bamboo skewers, 2 shrimp per skewer. Drizzle with olive oil and season with salt.

- Preheat barbecue to medium high: 375F (190C). Oil grill.

- Place the shrimp on the grill and put a sheet of foil under the exposed skewers to prevent burning.

- Grill one minute or until nicely caramelized and charred. Flip and baste with the reserved sauce. Shrimp are cooked when they just turn pink.

- Serve with extra basting sauce.

HAZELNUT CRUSTED HALIBUT WITH STRAWBERRY SALSA

Halibut was made for grilling. It has a nice firm flesh that holds up well on the BBQ and a nice sweet buttery flavour. In this recipe we bump up the texture by giving the fish a nutty crust. Check out this strawberry salsa. Easy to make and delicious on just about anything you grill, from fish to chicken (okay, maybe not a T-bone). Don't make the salsa too far in advance or the strawberries will become mushy. Serves 6

6 skinless halibut fillets, 6-oz (170 g)
     each 1 1/2 inches thick

1 tablespoon (15 ml) vegetable oil

Salt and pepper to taste

Crust:

1 cup (250 ml) finely chopped lightly
     toasted hazelnuts

2 tablespoons (30 ml) melted unsalted butter

Zest of 1 large lemon

Strawberry Salsa:

2 cups (500 ml) strawberries, cleaned
     and hulled

1/2 cup (125 ml) fresh mint leaves,
     roughly chopped

2 tablespoons (30 ml) finely diced red onion

2 tablespoons (30 ml) good quality
     balsamic vinegar

Freshly ground pepper and salt to taste

- Drizzle both sides of the fish with oil and season with salt and pepper.

- To make the salsa smash up the berries with a fork until chunky, or dice into small 1/8-inch (3 mm) pieces. Add the remaining salsa ingredients, stir to combine and season to taste with salt and pepper.

- For the crust, mix together the nuts with the melted butter and zest.

- Preheat barbecue to high: 475F–500F (246C–260C). Oil grill.

- Place the fish on the grill and grill for 4 minutes or until nice char marks are achieved. Flip the fish, top with nut mixture and continue to cook a further 3–4 minutes.

- Remove from grill and serve with strawberry salsa.

MISO CITRUS GRILLED SABLE FISH

This is one of my all time favourite fish recipes. It's amazing with any white fish if you can't find sable fish (also known as black cod). The fish becomes salty and tangy and develops an excellent golden colour. Ask your fishmonger to stock miso (a Japanese soybean based paste) and sable fish. If he's smart, he'll appreciate the suggestion. Sake is Japanese rice wine and ponzu sauce is like grown up soy. Serves 6

6 portions of fresh sable fish, 7 oz

(198 g) each

Miso citrus marinade:

1/4 cup (60 ml) sake

1/4 cup (60 ml) ponzu sauce

1/8 cup (30 ml) sugar

1/2 cup (125 ml) light miso paste

2 teaspoons (10 ml) fresh grated ginger

1/4 cup (60 ml) grape seed oil

Salt and pepper

Oil for brushing

- To make the marinade, combine the sake, ponzu and sugar in a large bowl. Whisk until the sugar is dissolved. Whisk in the miso until smooth. Add the ginger, then whisk in the oil gradually, to emulsify.

- Place the fish into a shallow pan and pour the marinade over. Place in the refrigerator for 2 hours.

- Remove from the marinade and season with salt and pepper.

- Preheat barbecue to high: 475F–500F (245C–260C). Oil grill well.

- Place fish on the oiled grill and cook for 4 minutes per side or until desired doneness.

- Serve hot.

When grilling fish:

- Make sure the fish is super fresh and firm.

- Clean and oil your grill well.

- Salt and oil the fish right before you're ready to grill.

- Don't mess with the fish – leave it to cook undisturbed.

- Have a great fish spatula that has thin steel and flexibility.

- Make sure the grills are hot hot hot.

HERB AND GARLIC GRILLED SHRIMP

This is such a simple recipe. It's perfect for a weeknight dinner with a salad or on top of some pasta with olive oil and Parmesan cheese. Rosemary and garlic is a classic combo for shrimp. Please, don't cook the shrimp for more than one minute a side. They really do cook that fast (the 21/25 size) and you'll end up with rubbery shrimp otherwise. Serves 4

20 shrimp (21/25) peeled and deveined

1 tablespoon (15 ml) chopped fresh garlic

1 tablespoon (15 ml) fresh chopped rosemary

1/4 cup (60 ml) chopped fresh parsley

1 teaspoon (5 ml) celery salt

1 tablespoon (15 ml) olive oil

Pepper to taste

Fresh lemon wedges, optional

- Place shrimp in a large sealable baggie. Add the rosemary, parsley, celery salt, garlic, olive oil and pepper. Swoosh the baggie around so all the shrimp are lightly coated with marinade. Refrigerate for 1 hour.

- Preheat grill to high: 475F–500F (245C-260C). Oil grill.

- Place shrimp directly on the grill and cook for 1 minute per side or until nicely charred and just turning pink.

- Remove from grill and serve hot with a drizzle of fresh lemon.

POWER PLAY CRAB CAKES WITH PEACH SALSA

We love crab cakes and this peach salsa/crab cake combo screams summer-time. You can use regular bread crumbs if you can't find Japanese panko and remember, always pick through the crabmeat before adding to the other ingredients. You're looking for little bits of shell which can do major dental work damage if you bite down on one. It doesn't happen very often but better safe than sorry, right? Yield: 20 portions

1 1/2 lb (680 g) crabmeat, picked over
　　for shells

1 cup (250 ml) fresh but firm bread crumbs
　　such as Japanese panko

1/4 cup (60 ml) finely chopped red bell pepper

1/2 cup (125 ml) finely chopped green onion

3 tablespoons (45 ml) mayonnaise

1 teaspoon (5 ml) Worcestershire sauce

2 teaspoons (10 ml) Cajun seasoning

2 teaspoons (10 ml) Dijon mustard

1 tablespoon (15 ml) roughly chopped
　　fresh dill

1 large egg, lightly beaten

Coating:

1 cup (250 ml) panko bread crumbs

3 tablespoons (45 ml) unsalted
　　melted butter

Peach Salsa (optional)
See page 256 or use store-bought

- To make cakes combine Dijon, dill, Worcestershire, mayonnaise, onion, red peppers and Cajun seasoning in a medium bowl. Add the crabmeat, egg and panko bread crumbs and mix well. Refrigerate to firm up.

- Divide the mixture into 20 equal portions and form into 2-inch (5 cm) rounds.

- Mix the melted butter with the panko in a shallow dish. Dip each cake in the crumb mixture to evenly coat.

- Preheat barbecue to medium: 350F (176C). Oil grill.

- Place the cakes over direct heat and cook, lid up, for 3–4 minutes or until the crumbs are nice and toasty and golden grill marks are achieved. Flip and continue to cook until both sides are crispy and golden.

- Remove from grill and serve with a spoonful of peach salsa.

SEAFOOD KABOBS

Horseradish, sugar and yogurt are the base of this funky unique marinade.
You can substitute any firm fleshed whitefish for the swordfish if you'd like.
I like to serve these kabobs with couscous and some sort of fruity chutney
(you're choice, there's a bunch listed in the Salsas & Chutneys chapter).
Yield: 8 kabobs

16 medium-sized scallops (10/20 count),
  cleaned and debearded

16 medium shrimp (16/20 count), peeled
  and deveined

2 fresh swordfish steaks, 1 1/2-inch-thick,
  cut into 1 1/2-inch cubes

Vegetable oil for brushing

8 8-inch bamboo skewers soaked in
  cool water for 30 minutes

Marinade:

1 cup (250 ml) whole fat plain yogurt

2 tablespoons (30 ml) horseradish

2 tablespoons (30 ml) fresh basil leaves,
  roughly chopped

1 tablespoon (15 ml) fresh lemon zest

1 tablespoon (15 ml) granulated white sugar

Salt and pepper to taste

- Skewer seafood onto bamboo skewers alternating ingredients, using two of each seafood per kabob.

- Place the kabobs in a large shallow dish.

- In a medium bowl combine the yogurt, horseradish, basil, sugar, lemon zest and pepper. Reserve a 1/4 cup (60 ml) of the mixture and pour the rest over the kabobs. Marinate in the refrigerator for 1 hour.

- Remove seafood from marinade and pat dry. Drizzle with oil and season with salt and pepper. Keep refrigerated until ready to grill.

- Preheat barbecue to medium high: 375F (190C). Oil grill.

- Place the kabobs on the grill and put a piece of tin foil under the exposed part of the skewers to prevent burning.

- Grill for 2 minutes per side or until nice golden char marks are achieved and shrimp are bright pink. Baste with the reserved marinade while cooking.

- Remove from grill and serve.

SPICY GRILLED TUNA STEAK WITH ORANGE MANGO SAUCE

The difference between fresh and canned tuna is night and day. It's the difference between grape juice and wine. Go to your fishmonger and ask for sushi-grade tuna. Notice how the fish is a deep purple-red like a beef steak. Cook it the same way you would beef – rare to medium rare (I like mine rare). Overcooked tuna turns ash grey and becomes dry and just all 'round bad. This recipe features a spicy rub that forms a nice crust when the fish hits the grill. Serves 6

6 fresh tuna steaks, 6 oz (170 g) each

Vegetable oil for brushing

Rub:

2 tablespoons (30 ml) ancho chili powder

2 teaspoons (10 ml) chili flakes

1 teaspoon (5 ml) ground cumin

2 teaspoons (10 ml) freshly ground
   black pepper

2 teaspoons (10 ml) kosher salt

Orange Mango sauce:

1 tablespoon (15 ml) unsalted butter

2 large, ripe mangos, peeled and
   roughly chopped

1 small red onion cut into 1/4-inch (6 mm) dice

1 jalapeno, seeded and diced

2 teaspoons (10 ml) minced fresh ginger

1 tablespoon (15 ml) Sambal or your
   favourite hot sauce

Juice of 3–4 limes

1 tablespoon (15 ml) frozen orange
   juice concentrate

Salt and pepper to taste

- To make the glaze, melt butter in large skillet set over medium-high heat. Add the ginger, onion, jalapeno and mango. Cook while stirring for 4 minutes or until onion is translucent and mango is very tender.

- Remove from heat and add the Sambal, lime juice and the orange juice concentrate. Cool slightly; place all ingredients in a blender and puree until smooth. Strain into a bowl and season with salt and pepper.

- In a small bowl combine the rub ingredients.

- Place the rub in a shallow large dish and press each tuna steak into the rub on one side only and drizzle lightly with oil.

- Preheat barbecue to medium high: 475F (245C). Oil grill.

- Place tuna steaks on grill for 2 minutes per side or until a nice crust forms. (Tuna is best served rare.)

- Remove from barbecue and serve immediately with Orange Mango Sauce.

WHOLE GRILLED SALMON WITH MUSTARD

It is always preferable to BBQ whole fish as the bones add extra flavour. Besides, it looks great. Your fishmonger will cut off the fins and scale the fish for you so there's no muss or fuss. You'll need to use a fish basket for this recipe (definitely worth the few bucks) as it makes turning the whole fish a fall-apart-proof operation. Imagine how good the leftovers are going to taste on some crusty bread the next day for lunch. Yield: 1 whole fish

1 whole 5 lb (2.26 kg) salmon, freshest
  available, scales and fins removed
1 bunch fresh dill
Zest of 2 lemons
2 tablespoons (30 ml) olive oil
Course sea salt and freshly ground pepper

Garlic butter:

1/2 cup (125 ml) unsalted butter
2 teaspoons (10 ml) minced garlic

Mustard sauce:

1 1/2 cups (625 ml) sour cream
1 1/2 tablespoons (22 ml) grainy Dijon mustard
1 tablespoon (15 ml) freshly chopped dill
1 1/2 tablespoons (22 ml) fresh lemon juice
Salt and pepper to taste

- To make the sauce, combine all the ingredients in a medium bowl and whisk to combine. Season with salt and pepper.

- Melt butter in a small saucepan set over low heat, skim off the foam that rises to the surface. Add the chopped garlic and simmer until garlic is fragrant. Remove from heat.

- Season the cavity of the fish with salt and pepper. Sprinkle with lemon zest and drizzle with olive oil. Brush the outside of the fish with olive oil and liberally sprinkle with salt.

- Preheat barbecue to medium high: 375F (190C). Preheat a flat fish grill basket for 15 minutes.

- Place the whole fish in the grilling basket and cook for 10 minutes with the lid down. Carefully flip the fish and continue to cook the fish another 10 minutes.

- Brush the outside of the fish with garlic butter in the last 5 minutes of cooking.

- Remove fish when skin is crispy and fish is medium rare. Note: A fish of this size will continue cooking after it has been removed from the grill.

- Serve with lemon wedges and mustard sauce.

VEGGIES, SALADS and SIDES

BBQ just isn't BBQ without some excellent side dishes
and nothing screams summertime like a big fresh
salad. There was a time when no self-respecting
carnivore would be caught dead with a salad. There
was also a time when people thought smoking
cigarettes was cool and the earth was flat.
Things change.

I'm particularly gaga about the Sweet Potato Fries
with Chipotle Mayo and the Blue Cheese and
Bacon Potato Salad. Enjoy!

BLACK MAGIC FIGS

We love Mission figs (introduced to California by Franciscan missionaries). We think they're the sweetest and are just the right size. That being said, any ripe fig will do if there aren't any Mission figs around. First you marinate the figs in rich boozy port, then wrap them in salty prosciutto and grill till the ham is crisp and the figs have warmed through. Serve them on their own as an appetizer or in the middle of a big bowl of greens or as a side to a nice piece of grilled chicken. Yield: 15 figs

15 fresh black Mission figs

2 cups port wine (500 ml)

Fresh ground pepper to taste

7–8 sheets of thinly sliced Italian prosciutto

- Using a small sharp knife score the figs at the bottom making a large x shape.

- Place the port in a large bowl and stir in the pepper. Add the figs and marinate for 1 hour.

- Carefully strain the figs over a saucepan set over medium-low heat and warm the port. Simmer for 20 minutes or until slightly thickened.

- Cut the prosciutto slices in half lengthwise. Wrap the prosciutto around the figs. If necessary secure with a toothpick. Place on an oiled tray.

- Preheat barbecue to medium high: 375F (190C). Oil grill.

- Place the figs on the grill, turning frequently to prevent burning, until the prosciutto is golden brown and slightly crispy.

- Remove from grill and serve drizzled with the reduced sauce.

BLUE CHEESE AND BACON POTATO SALAD

You serve this potato salad warm. Assemble all the ingredients and pull the potatoes off the grill just before serving. Not all blue cheese is super stinky and sharp. You can get some milder and creamier varieties if your taste leans that way. Try to find yourself a good cheese monger who'll spend the time to explain the different tastes and textures of the cheese he sells. A good one will let you try samples. Serves 6–8

3 lb (1.36 kg) red skinned potatoes,
    cooked not cooled

1/2 lb (226 g) bacon, cooked and drained

1 cup (250 ml) red onion, thinly sliced

8 oz (226g) good blue cheese

1/4 cup (60 ml) fresh basil leaves
    roughly chopped

1 big bunch watercress, stems trimmed

Salt and pepper may be added but do
    taste before adding

Dressing:

1 tablespoon (15 ml) cider vinegar

1 teaspoon (5 ml) Dijon mustard

1 tablespoon (15 ml) fresh lemon juice

2 teaspoons (10 ml) minced fresh garlic

1/4 cup (60 ml) olive oil

Pepper to taste

- In a small bowl or jar mix together all dressing ingredients until well combined.

- Cut warm potatoes into medium chunks, place in a large bowl and cover with dressing.

- Add the remaining ingredients and toss gently to combine.

PEAR AND FENNEL SALAD

BBQ'd salad . . . go figure. Fennel has a mild licorice taste and plays nicely off the sweet crunchy pear and the peppery watercress. I also like doing this one with arugula and a bit of creamy blue cheese. Try squeezing an orange or two for the juice into the dressing. Trust me, it'll make a huge difference.

Yield: 6 Servings

2 medium sized fennel bulbs cut into 4–6
*   slices about 1/4 inch (6 mm) thick*
2 large ripe Bosc pears, peeled and
*   quartered, core removed*
1 tablespoon (15 ml) fruity olive oil
2 bunch fresh watercress, washed and dried,
*   approximately 2 cups (500 ml)*
Salt and pepper to taste

Dressing:

1/4 cup (60 ml) sherry vinegar
1/2 cup (125 ml) orange juice
1 tablespoon (15 ml) brown sugar
1/3 cup (83 ml) olive oil
Salt and pepper to taste

- Place all dressing ingredients into a small jar with a lid. Shake vigorously until combined. Season to taste with salt and pepper.

- Preheat barbecue to medium: 350F (176C). Oil grill.

- Coat the fennel and pear slices with the olive oil and season with salt and pepper.

- Place fennel on grill, cook on one side for 4–5 minutes or until golden char marks and deep caramelization are achieved. Flip and continue to cook the fennel for 4 more minutes.

- Add the pears. Turn them after 2–3 minutes or until nice golden char marks appear and pears are slightly softened. Repeat on the other side.

- Remove fennel and pears from grill and drizzle with sherry vinaigrette. Immediately toss with the watercress and more of the vinaigrette to taste.

BUMPER CROP TOMATO SALAD

Nothing says summer like fresh tomatoes and mercifully, local markets are starting to offer all sorts and sizes and colours and tastes (there are dozens of varieties of tomatoes). Tomatoes are part of the nightshade family along with tobacco and eggplant (useless trivia for your next dinner party). Here's our take on a classic tomato salad featuring red onion, basil and bocconcini cheese (fresh mozzarella). Notice there's no vinegar in the recipe. That's because you get all the tartness you need from the juicy tomatoes. Serves 6

8 summer tomatoes cut into wedges
   (use a variety of colour and sizes)
1/4 of a small red onion, sliced very thin
1/4 cup (60 ml) fresh basil leaves, torn
9 baby bocconcini balls sliced 1/4-inch
   (6-mm) thick
2 tablespoons (30 ml) good quality olive oil
Salt and pepper to taste (use a good
   quality salt)

- Place the tomatoes on a large serving platter. Sprinkle with onions, basil and cheese. Drizzle with olive oil and season with salt and pepper.

- That's it.

BBQ'D YORKSHIRE PUDDING

This one goes great with the Prime Rib roast on page 28. Your guests will flip when you serve them BBQ'd Yorkshire Pudding. You use the drippings from the roast pan and make the puddings while your roast is resting under tin foil. Yield: 12 large muffin cup puddings

6 large eggs

2 1/4 cups (560 ml) cold whole milk

1 teaspoon (5 ml) salt

1/2 teaspoon (2.5 ml) fresh ground pepper

2 cups (500 ml) sifted all-purpose flour

1/4 cup (60 ml) pan drippings from
*   a roast beef*

Note: *if you run shy of drippings, vegetable*
*   oil or melted duck fat can be substituted.*

- Place eggs, milk, salt, and pepper in a large bowl and whisk to mix. Whisk in the flour and 2 table-spoons of the drippings. Cover and chill for 30 minutes.

- Prepare barbecue for indirect medium heat: 400–425F (205-218C). Leave one of the burners (large enough for your muffin tin) off. Leave all other burners on high.

- Preheat the muffin tin for 5 minutes.

- Add the remaining drippings to a preheated muffin tin, about 3/4 teaspoon (3.75 ml) per tin. Heat the drippings for 1 minute. Pour the batter into the hot muffin tins (about 3/4 full) and close lid.

- Cook until puffed and brown, about 20 minutes. Don't open the lid to peek, as the temperature has to be constant for the batter to puff.

- Remove and serve with Herbed Smoked Prime Rib of Beef.

CHILLED SUMMER PEACH SOUP

This is one of my two favourite summer soups (the other is a chilled smoked salmon soup found in the Great Canadian Food Show Cookbook available at knight-tv.com). It's cold and tart and tangy and sweet all at once. You can buy crystallized ginger in most health food or bulk food stores.

Serves 6 as an appetizer

6 large, ripe peaches

1 tablespoon (15 ml) honey

1 cup (250 ml) plain yogurt

1/4 cup (60 ml) peach nectar

1/4 cup (60 ml) Riesling white wine

1 tablespoon (15 ml) minced
   crystallized ginger

1 tablespoon (15 ml) chopped fresh mint

1 tablespoon (15 ml) chopped fresh chives

1/2 teaspoon (2.5 ml) orange zest

1 teaspoon (5 ml) five-spice powder

Garnish:

1 cup fresh raspberries (250 ml)

1/4 cup plain yogurt (60 ml)

Mint sprigs

- Place peaches in boiling water for 1 minute. Remove and place in an ice-water bath. Gently pull off the skin. Halve and pit peaches.

- In a blender, puree peaches, honey, yogurt, nectar, wine, crystallized ginger, mint, chives, orange zest and five-spice powder. Refrigerate, covered for 2 hours.

- Taste and adjust sweetness level, adding a little more yogurt to make sure that the soup is not so sweet.

- Ladle into soup bowls and garnish with mint sprigs, a small dollop of yogurt, and 4 raspberries per bowl placed on top of the yogurt.

Five-spice powder is a combination of cinnamon, star anise, fennel, cloves and Szechwan pepper.

DOUBLE HIT SMOKED NUTS

Bet you don't think nuts when you think BBQ, right? Well check this recipe out. First you coat the nuts in a bunch of spices and then you smoke them over chicory wood. Way better than anything you'd ever buy in a store and they're really easy to make. Yield: 3 cups (750 ml)

3 cups (750 ml) mixed raw nuts such as
   almonds, cashew, hazelnuts, pecans

1 teaspoon (5 ml) ground cinnamon

1 tablespoon (15 ml) ground cayenne pepper

1 teaspoon (5 ml) ground cumin

2 teaspoon (10 ml) paprika

1 teaspoon (5 ml) ground coriander

1/2 teaspoon (2.5 ml) thyme

1 1/2 tablespoons (22.5 ml) kosher salt

2 tablespoons (30 ml) lightly packed
   brown sugar

2 tablespoons (30 ml) melted unsalted butter

2 egg whites

6 cups (1.5 L) hickory wood chips, 4 of the
   cups (1 L) soaked in cool water for 1 hour

- Place nuts on a large ovenproof baking tray and drizzle evenly with butter.

- In a medium bowl mix together the spices with salt and sugar until evenly combined. Toss the nuts with the sugar and spices until evenly coated

- Whip the egg until just frothy in a medium bowl. Gently mix all the spiced nuts with the frothed egg white.

- Make 2 smoke pouches (see page 37).

- Prepare barbecue for indirect smoking: 220 F (104 C). Place one burner on high and the other off. Place the smoke pouch on the burner with heat, close lid and wait for smoke. Adjust heat on the barbecue if necessary.

- Place the nuts over the indirect side of the barbecue.

- Smoke the nuts for 1 hour or until the nuts are crispy and golden brown. Change the smoke pouch when smoke dissipates.

- Remove from the barbecue and place on a parchment-lined tray to cool.

GRILLED ASPARAGUS TWO WAYS

Here are two really simple ways to serve grilled asparagus, one hot and one cold. Serves 6

30 asparagus spears, trimmed of woody stock

3 tablespoons (45 ml) olive oil

Sat and pepper

#1 (serve hot)

2 teaspoons fresh thyme, chopped and
   stems removed

1/2 cup (125 ml) room temperature butter

Zest of one lemon

Salt and pepper

#2 (serve cold)

3 tablespoons (45 ml) toasted pine nuts

1/2 cup (125 ml) crumbled feta cheese

Juice of 1 lemon

- In a small bowl mix together butter, lemon zest, thyme, salt and pepper.

- Place the butter on a piece of plastic wrap and roll into a log shape the diameter of a silver dollar. Chill the butter for 30 minutes or until firm enough to cut.

- Preheat grill to high: 475F–500F (246C–260C). Oil grill.

- Place asparagus on a tray, drizzle with oil and sprinkle with salt and pepper.

- Place the asparagus on the grill and grill for 1–2 minutes (depending on size) or until the asparagus turns bright green and has golden char marks. Turn the asparagus all the while you cook. Remove from grill and divide the asparagus into 2 bunches.

- Slice the chilled butter into rounds and place on top of 1/2 of the hot grilled asparagus. Serve.

- Refrigerate the remaining asparagus for 30 minutes until well chilled. Remove from the refrigerator and top with pine nuts, feta cheese and finish with a squeeze of fresh lemon juice.

CRISPY GINGER SLAW

Tired of the same old slaw? Here's one with an Asian twist. I like my slaw slightly chilled as it adds crispiness. Serves 6

2 cups (500 ml) Napa cabbage,
    finely shredded

1 cup (250 ml) shredded carrot

1 cup (250 ml) snow peas, sliced thin
    or slivered

1/2 cup (125 ml) thinly sliced yellow pepper

1/2 cup (125 ml) thinly sliced red pepper

1/2 cup (125 ml) fresh bean sprouts, rinsed

2 tablespoons (30 ml) cilantro

2 tablespoons (30 ml) lightly toasted
    sesame seeds

Dressing:

1/4 cup (60 ml) soy sauce

1/4 cup (60 ml) rice vinegar

3 tablespoons (45 ml) light sesame oil

3 tablespoons (45 ml) vegetable oil

2 tablespoons (30 ml) white sugar

2 tablespoons (30 ml) mirin

1 teaspoon (5 ml) minced garlic

1 tablespoon (15 ml) fresh minced ginger

1 tablespoon (15 ml) fresh lime juice

1/4 teaspoon (1.25 ml) cayenne pepper

- For the dressing in a small bowl, whisk together soy sauce, rice vinegar, sesame oil, vegetable oil, sugar, mirin, garlic, ginger, lime juice and cayenne. Cover and refrigerate for 4 hours to blend flavours.

- In a large bowl, combine cabbage, carrots, snow peas, peppers and bean sprouts. Toss to mix. Add the dressing and toss to distribute evenly. Garnish with fresh chopped cilantro and sesame seeds.

GRILLED BEET, CARROT AND FENNEL SALAD

Make sure you wear rubber gloves when you handle the beets or you'll end up with very stained hands. Grilling caramelizes the natural sugars in the veggies (that's how you get the char marks) and sweetens them up. The dressing has a nice Asian pop to it. Serves 6

3 medium fresh beets peeled and sliced
    into 1/4 inch rounds
4 medium carrots, halved lengthwise
8 thin slices of fresh fennel, held together
    at core
1 tablespoon (15 ml) olive oil
Salt and pepper to taste

Dressing:

2 green onions finely diced, white part only
2 tablespoons (30 ml) peanut oil
1 teaspoon (5 ml) sesame oil
2 tablespoons (30 ml) rice wine vinegar
2 teaspoons (10 ml) soy sauce
1 teaspoon (5 ml) fresh grated ginger
Pinch of dried chili flakes
2 teaspoons (10 ml) fresh lemon juice
4 cups (1 L) baby romaine lettuce,
    washed and dried
2 tablespoons (30 ml) chopped fresh
    cilantro leaves
2 tablespoons (30 ml) toasted sesame seeds
Salt and pepper to taste

- Place the beets, carrots and fennel on a baking sheet. Drizzle with olive oil and season with salt and pepper.

- Preheat barbecue to medium high: 375F (190C). Oil barbecue grill.

- Place the beets, carrots and fennel on grill for 2–4 minutes per side or until golden char marks are achieved and the vegetables are still slightly firm to touch. Remove from grill and cool.

- Place all dressing ingredients in a medium sized Mason jar and shake vigorously until combined.

- Chop the now cooled vegetables into thin strips and place in a medium bowl. Toss the vegetables with the dressing to evenly coat.

- Divide the romaine leaves into 4–6 bowls equally. Top with the grilled vegetables equally and sprinkle with cilantro and sesame seeds.

GRILLED CORN ON THE COB WRAPPED IN BACON

Yield: 12 half cobs

*6 cobs of fresh corn, husked and cut
    in half widthwise*

12 slices of bacon

Salt and pepper

12 sturdy toothpicks

Drip pan

- Season corn with salt and pepper.

- Wrap the bacon around the half cob of corn securing with a toothpick.

- Place a drip pan under the grates of barbecue.

- Prepare barbecue for direct medium heat: 350F (175C). Oil grill.

- Place wrapped corn on grates over drip pan.

- Cook a few minutes turning. Close the lid of the barbecue and cook 2–3 minutes. Open lid and move the corn around to create even browning and crisping of the bacon.

- Do this for about 8 minutes until all the bacon is crisp and corn is cooked.

- Remove from barbecue and serve immediately.

GRILLED CORN WITH ORANGE BUTTER

You have to keep the husk on the corn to keep it from burning but you take out all that pesky silk that lies between the husk and the corn itself.

Yield: 6 corn cobs

6 fresh ears of corn

1/2 cup (125 ml) room temperature
  unsalted butter

1 tablespoon (15 ml) orange zest

Salt and pepper

- In a small bowl combine the butter, orange zest, salt and pepper. Place the butter on a large piece of plastic wrap and roll into a cylinder shape. Place into the refrigerator to set up for 30 minutes.

- Remove the corn the silk from each cob but keep the husks on. Submerge corn in a large container of cool water and allow to soak for 1 hour.

- Remove from the water and shake off excess water.

- Prepare barbecue for medium-high direct grilling: 375F (190C). Oil the grill.

- Place corn on the grill and cover the barbecue. Turn cobs twice for 4–5 minutes or until you hear sputtering and the husks are nice and charred.

- Remove from grill and cool a few minutes. Using a towel grasp the ear and pull down the husk.

- Slice the butter into rounds and place on top of the corn.

GRILLED CUBANELLE PEPPERS STUFFED WITH CHEESE

Chill. You know what a Cubanelle or Anaheim pepper is. It's those big long skinny green ones. They have a wee bit of heat but are very mild and perfect for stuffing. We use jalapeno jack cheese but you could go with a cheddar/mozzarella combo. Two of these makes a perfect vegetarian main dish. Yield: 12 portions

6 Cubanelle or Anaheim chilies, cut in half
  lengthwise, seeds and veins removed

1/2 cup (125 ml) goat cheese crumbled

1 cup (250 ml) shredded jalapeno jack cheese

3 tablespoons (45 ml) roughly chopped
  cilantro leaves

1/4 cup (60 ml) thinly sliced scallions

1/2 cup (125 ml) roasted corn (see page 200)

Salt and pepper to taste

Olive oil for brushing

- In a medium bowl mix together the cheeses, cilantro, corn and scallions; season to taste with salt and pepper.

- Place the cut peppers on a tray and brush the outside with olive oil. Spoon the cheese mixture equally into the hollowed peppers.

- Preheat barbecue to medium: 350F (175C).

- Place a grill screen on the barbecue to preheat for 10 minutes. Oil grill screen.

- Place peppers on the oiled grill screen cheese-side up. Close the lid and cook the peppers until they are nicely charred and cheese is golden brown and bubbling.

- Remove from grill and cool slightly. Serve warm.

GRILLED CHICKEN AND PEACH SALAD

I actually prefer this salad cold so make the chicken in advance and stick it in the fridge for a while. If you're not big on spinach then substitute arugula. Either way, it makes a great lunch all on its own. Serves 6

4 boneless skinless chicken breast halves

Salt and pepper

1 teaspoon (5 ml) garlic powder

1 teaspoon (5 ml) onion powder

1 tablespoon (15 ml) olive oil

2 peaches pitted, one peeled and one
   with skin left on

2 celery stalks chopped fine

1/2 cup (125 ml) sliced toasted almonds

1/2 cup (125 ml) mayonnaise

4 cups (1 L) washed and dried baby
   spinach leaves

Dressing:

1 tablespoon (15 ml) pure peach preserves

2 tablespoons (30 ml) white wine vinegar

2 teaspoons (10 ml) Dijon mustard

1/2 teaspoon (2.5 ml) fresh grated ginger

1/4 cup (60 ml) freshly squeezed orange juice

Salt and pepper to taste

- Rinse and pat dry chicken and place on a baking tray. Sprinkle both sides with onion and garlic powders and salt and pepper. Drizzle chicken with olive oil.

- Preheat barbecue to medium high: 375F (190C). Oil grill.

- Place chicken on the grill and cook for 5–6 minutes per side or until chicken has golden brown char marks and is cooked through.

- Remove chicken from grill, cover loosely with foil, let rest for 10 minutes then refrigerate until completely cool.

- Cut chicken into 1/2-inch (1.3 cm) cubes and place in a medium bowl. Add mayonnaise, chopped celery and the toasted almonds and mix to combine.

- Chop the peeled peach into bite-sized pieces, add to the chicken mixture and gently toss. Refrigerate until ready to use.

- Place all the dressing ingredients in a small Mason jar and shake vigorously to combine.

- Gently toss desired amount of the dressing with spinach and divide onto 6 chilled plates. Top the spinach with the chicken mixture.

- Garnish the salad with thin slices of the unpeeled peach.

GRILLED HARVEST VEGETABLES WITH MUSTARD GLAZE

The secret to doing mixed vegetables on the grill is figuring out how long each one takes to cook and then adding them in order so that they're all ready at the same time. And we've done that for you. The mustard glaze at the end adds a nice bite to your veggies. Serves 6

1/4 cup (60 ml) olive oil

Salt and pepper

1/4 cup (60 ml) Dijon mustard

1/4 cup (60 ml) good quality liquid honey

1 tablespoon (15 ml) fresh summer savory, roughly chopped

1 teaspoon (5 ml) Worcestershire sauce

1 bunch carrots, cut in half lengthwise or left whole, depending on size

1 butternut squash, peeled and cut into 2-inch (5-cm) chunks.

2 small rutabaga (turnip) peeled and cut into 1/2-inch (1.3-cm) rounds

2 Spanish onions, cut in quarters leaving the root intact

4 shallots, peeled and cut in half lengthwise

4 parsnips, each cut in half lengthwise

12 baby potatoes, cut in half

- In a medium bowl, whisk together the mustard, honey, oil, Worcestershire, savory, salt and pepper.

- Preheat barbecue to medium: 350F (176C). Oil the grill.

- Place the cut vegetables on a tray and drizzle with olive oil just to coat. Place all vegetables directly on the grill and cook until they just begin to have char marks, turning frequently to prevent burning.

- The carrots, parsnips and butternut squash will take 5–6 minutes while the rutabaga, onion and shallots will take about 10 minutes.

- Brush all with the mustard glaze. Cook until the glaze begins to bubble around the edges of the vegetables, about 2 minutes. Turn the vegetables and brush again with glaze. Cook a further minute.

- Remove from grill and brush again with the mustard mix.

GRILLED POTATO SKINS

Once upon a time people threw potato skins out. But not anymore. Make sure you get russet or baking potatoes because they have a thicker skin. Provolone is a semi-hard Italian cheese available in most grocery stores these days. You can go with just the cheddar or substitute mozzarella if you'd like. Serve one of these with a big honkin' steak. Yield: 12 potato halves

Large russet potatoes, skin on and washed

2 tablespoons (30 ml) olive oil

2 cups (500 ml) mixed grated cheese
   provolone and cheddar

1 cup (250 ml) cooked crispy bacon,
   drained and crumbled

1/2 cup (125 ml) sliced green onion

1/2 cup (125 ml) sour cream

Salt and pepper to taste

Optional garnish: salsa

- Prepare barbecue to medium-low indirect heat: 325F (162C). Leave 2 burners on medium and one burner off.

- Rub potatoes with 1 tablespoon (15 ml) of the olive oil and prick all over with a fork. This will stop a potato explosion and the olive oil will aid in crisping up the skin.

- Oil grill. Place potatoes over indirect heat for 40–50 minutes or until the potatoes are fully cooked. Remove from the grill and cool.

- Using a sharp serrated knife, slice the potato lengthwise in half. With a spoon, scoop out the insides leaving a 1/2-inch (1.3-cm) border of potato flesh on the skin. Season cavity with salt and pepper and drizzle with oil, paying close attention to the rim of the potato (the flesh border).

- Sprinkle cheese and bacon equally among the potatoes.

- Preheat barbecue to medium high, 375F (190C). Oil grill.

- Place potato skins cheese-side up on the grill. Close the lid and allow to cook for 7–8 minutes or until the cheese is bubbling and the skin is crispy.

- Remove from barbecue. Top with scallions, sour cream and salsa if desired.

GRILLED VEGETABLE QUESADILLA

Quesadillas are sort of Mexican fast food. Think great grilled veggies held together with melted cheese between two soft tortillas and cut into wedges. Perfect finger food for cocktail parties. You can add sliced chicken if you want to go carnivore. Serves 6

2 yellow peppers, quartered and seeded

2 orange peppers, quartered and seeded

1 red pepper, quarter and seeded

2 zucchini, sliced lengthwise 1/4-inch
    (6-mm) thick

1 red onion, cut in wedges

2 tablespoons (30 ml) chopped fresh
    basil (optional)

2 tablespoons (30 ml) olive oil

Salt and pepper to taste

5 oz (150g) grated mozzarella cheese

5 oz (150g) Monterey Jack cheese

12 soft tortillas

Oil for brushing

- Preheat barbecue to medium high: 375F (190C).

- Place all cut vegetables in a large bow and drizzle with olive oil, salt and pepper, coating all the vegetables well.

- Oil the grill. Place the peppers skin-side down; zucchini and onion directly on grill. Cook for approximately 2–3 minutes per side or until nice golden char marks are achieved. Note the onion will take a few minutes longer on each side.

- Remove from grill and toss with fresh basil. Once cooled, cut up the vegetables into bite-sized pieces.

- Place the flour tortilla on cutting board and lightly oil both sides. Sprinkle the cheese evenly between the 6 oiled tortilla shells, keeping a 1-inch (1.3-cm) border around the edges.

- Top cheese with vegetable mixture. Top with an oiled tortilla. Place all quesadillas onto a baking tray.

- Preheat barbecue to medium high: 375F (190C). Oil grill.

- Place each quesadilla directly on grill and cook for 2–3 minutes or until cheese is gooey and the tortilla is nice and crispy on one side. Flip using a hamburger flipper; cook the remaining side 2-3 minutes.

- Remove from grill. Let the quesadillas cool slightly and cut into equal triangles like a pizza.

- Serve with sour cream or guacamole if desired.

GRILLED VEGETABLE SALAD WITH GOAT CHEESE CROSTINI

We pretty much just went down to our local farmer's market and bought everything in sight to put this recipe together. You can and should vary it depending on what's in season wherever you are. Serves 6

1 red bell pepper, quartered lengthwise
   and seeded

1 yellow bell pepper, quartered lengthwise
   and seeded

1 bunch of rapini (2 handfuls)

1 zucchini, sliced lengthwise 1/4 inch
   (6 mm) thick

1 Japanese eggplant, sliced lengthwise
   1/4 inch (6 mm) thick

3 new potatoes, boiled and sliced 1/4 inch
   (6 mm) thick

1 small butternut squash peeled, seeded
   sliced into 1/4 inch (6 mm) slices

2 tablespoons (30 ml) fresh chopped basil

2 tablespoons (30 ml) fresh chopped oregano

Salt and pepper

Olive oil for drizzling

For the dressing:

- In a blender, combine the vinegar, onion, honey and Dijon and puree. With the motor running, slowly add the oil until it has emulsified. Season to taste with salt and pepper.

For the vegetables:

- Preheat barbecue to medium high: 475F (245C). Oil grill.

- Blanch the rapini in a large pot of boiling water for approximately 1 minute or until it turns bright green. Immediately place in an ice bath. Chill completely then pat dry.

Dressing:

3 tablespoons (45 ml) balsamic vinegar

1 tablespoon (15 ml) minced red onion

1 tablespoon (15 ml) finely chopped

green onion (white part only)

2 teaspoons (10 ml) Dijon mustard

2 teaspoons (10 ml) honey

1/2 cup (125 ml) olive oil

Salt and pepper

Goat Cheese Crostini:

6 slices French bread cut 1/2 inch

(1.3 cm) thick

6 slices of goat cheese, 1/4 inch

(1.3 cm) thick

2 teaspoons (10 ml) fresh thyme leaves

Salt and pepper

Olive oil for brushing

4 cups (1L) mesclun greens or your

favourite salad green

- Place all the chopped vegetables in a bowl and toss with herbs, olive oil and season with salt and pepper.

- Place vegetables on the grill and grill for 2 1/2 minutes per side or until nice golden brown char marks are achieved. The rapini will take only 1 minute per side.

- Remove from grill. Cool slightly and roughly chop the larger vegetables.

- Place in a large bowl and toss with 1/4 cup (60 ml) of dressing. Reserve.

For the crostini:

- Brush both sides of the bread slices with olive oil and place on the preheated grill. Grill for 1 minute per side or until the bread is golden and crisp. Top each bread slice with goat cheese and sprinkle with thyme and salt and pepper.

- Divide the mesclun greens between 6 plates and drizzle with desired amount of the dressing. Top each with grilled vegetables and garnish with a goat cheese crostini.

MESQUITE SMOKED TOMATO BRUSCHETTA

Bruschetta is a nice starter for any meal and smoking the tomatoes gives it an extra kick. Don't skip the step where you rub garlic on the bread. Might not seem like much but it really adds tons of flavour. Serves 6–8

6 ripe tomatoes, washed, quartered
  and seeded

1 teaspoon (5 ml) dried chili flakes

2 cloves garlic, thinly sliced

1 sprig of fresh thyme

2 shallots sliced thin

1 tablespoon (15 ml) olive oil

Salt and pepper to taste

Assembly:

1/2 cup (125 ml) fresh basil leaves, torn

Splash of balsamic vinegar but not
  necessary if tomatoes are perfect and ripe

1 tablespoon (15 ml), good quality olive oil

 Salt and pepper

1 nice baguette sliced into 1/4 inch
  (6 mm) rounds

2 whole garlic cloves cut in half

3 cups (750 ml) mesquite wood chips; 2 cups
  (500 ml) of the chips soaked in cool water
  for 1 hour and drained.

- Seed tomatoes by cutting in quarters and using a small paring knife remove the seeds.

- Drizzle the tomatoes with olive oil, salt, pepper and sprinkle the thyme, garlic slices and shallots evenly over tomatoes.

- Make a smoke pouch (see page 37).

- Prepare barbecue for indirect smoking leaving one burner on high and the other burners off. Place smoke pouch on burner that is on, close lid and wait for smoke.

- Reduce heat if necessary to 220F (104C).

- Once smoke is achieved place the tomatoes over indirect heat. Close lid and smoke for 15–20 minutes or until slightly (very slightly) dried. The idea is to smoke them without overcooking them and having their texture lost.

- Remove from grill. Slip skins off of the tomatoes with your hands and cut into bite-sized pieces. Place in a bowl and add the chopped basil, olive oil and salt and pepper and mix. Chill the mixture.

- For the bread slices, preheat barbecue to medium high: 375F (190C). Oil grill.

- Place bread slices on grill until golden brown, about 1 minute per side. Remove from grill and rub with halved garlic cloves.

- Spoon the smoked tomato filling over crispy bread slices.

ROASTED SUMMER BEET SALAD

Make sure you wear a new pair of rubber gloves when you're peeling and slicing the beets otherwise you'll stain your hands. You can substitute a milder creamy blue cheese for the goat cheese if you'd like. Squeezing the orange juice (as opposed to out of a carton) makes all the difference in the dressing. Serves 6–8

Beets:

8 large red beets or if available mixed
    coloured beets of the same size

2 tablespoons (30 ml) olive oil

Salt and pepper to taste

Salad:

1/2 cup (125 ml) thinly sliced red onion

1/4 cup (60 ml) balsamic vinegar

1/2 cup (125 ml) olive oil

Juice of one orange

1 cup (250 ml) crumbled goat cheese

2 tablespoons (30 ml) fresh basil

Salt and pepper

2/3 cup (165 ml) toasted walnuts

- Remove the tops from the beets. Using tines of a fork, pierce beets all over. Drizzle with the oil and salt and pepper.

- Prepare barbecue for indirect low heat: 245F (118C). Leave one side on medium low and the other side off.

- Place beets over indirect heat and cook until slightly soft when pierced with a fork – about 1 1/2 hours. Remove.

- In a bowl combine the olive oil, balsamic vinegar, orange juice and salt and pepper. Whisk until well combined.

- When beets are cool enough to handle slip the skins off and cut into 1/2 inch (1.3 cm) rounds.

- Place in a bowl, drizzle with dressing and add the basil and red onion. Sprinkle with the goat cheese and top with walnuts.

SKILLET CORN BREAD

Serves 6–8

5 tablespoons (75 ml) unsalted butter

1 1/3 cups (333 ml) yellow stone-ground
  cornmeal

3/4 cup (187 ml) all purpose white flour

2 1/2 tablespoons (22.5 ml) white
  granulated sugar

1 tablespoon (15 ml) salt

1 tablespoon (15 ml) baking powder

1/2 teaspoon (2.5 ml) baking soda

1 cup (250 ml) buttermilk

1 large egg

1 teaspoon (5 ml) finely chopped
  jalapeno pepper

1/2 cup (125 ml) chopped scallion,
  white parts only

1 cup (250 ml) fresh corn kernels

- Preheat oven to 425F (218C).

- In a small saucepan, melt 4 tablespoons (60 ml) of butter. Remove from heat.

- Place the remaining tablespoon (15 ml) of butter into a round 9-inch (23 cm) cast iron pan and heat in the oven while preparing the batter.

- In a medium bowl, sift the cornmeal, flour, sugar, salt, baking powder, and soda. In another bowl, whisk the buttermilk, egg and the melted butter together. Add to the cornmeal mixture and stir just to combine. Stir in the scallions, corn and jalapeno.

- Take the hot pan from the oven and tilt it to distribute the melted butter. Immediately pour the batter into the pan.

- Bake for about 20 minutes, or until a cake tester (toothpick) inserted into the centre comes out clean.

- Remove from oven and let cool slightly before cutting.

SOUTHWESTERN POTATO SALAD

This is one spud salad that tastes way better at room temperature or warm, bringing out the flavours in the dressing. You can boil the potatoes and make the dressing a few hours in advance and leave everything covered on the counter till you assemble the salad. Serves 6–8

4 lb (1.81 kg) small red new potatoes

1 red pepper seeded, sliced 1/4 inch
    (6 mm) thick

1 yellow pepper seeded, sliced 1/4 inch
    (6 mm) thick

1 cup (250 ml) halved cherry tomatoes

Dressing:

1 jalapeno pepper, stemmed and seeded

2 cloves of garlic, crushed

1/2 tablespoon (7.5 ml) sugar

2 teaspoons (10 ml) minced fresh ginger

1/2 cup (125 ml) pine nuts, roasted

Zest of 1 lemon

1 cup (250 ml) extra virgin olive oil

1/2 cup (125 ml) fresh basil leaves

1/2 cup (125 ml) mint leaves

1/4 cup (125 ml) fresh cilantro leaves

- To make the dressing, combine the chilies, garlic, sugar, ginger, nuts, lemon zest and 1/2 cup (125 ml) of the olive oil in a blender or food processor. Process until smooth.

- Add the basil, mint, and cilantro and blend, while slowly adding the rest of the oil until a thick puree is achieved. Season with salt and pepper. The dressing will keep for 1 week in a sealed container in the refrigerator.

- Steam or boil the potatoes until just tender. Cool slightly and cut in halves.

- Place in a large bowl and pour desired amount of dressing (about 1/2 cup) over the potatoes while they are still warm. Stir in peppers and tomatoes.

- Serve at room temperature or warm.

SOUTHWESTERN SWEET POTATO FRIES WITH CHIPOTLE MAYONNAISE

Sweet potato fries won't crisp up the way spuds do, but man are they good eating – plus they go with just about everything. Chipotles are just smoked jalapenos smothered in a spicy tomato-based sauce called adobo. You can find them in pretty much any grocery store these days. Enjoy. Serves 6

4 sweet potatoes, washed but not peeled

2 teaspoons lime juice (10 ml)

1 1/2 tablespoon olive oil (22.5 ml)

1 teaspoon salt or more to taste (5 ml)

1/2 teaspoon fresh ground pepper (2.5 ml)

1/2 teaspoons ground cumin (2.5 ml)

Chipotle mayonnaise

1 cup (250 ml) whole egg mayonnaise

2 chipotle chilies in adobo sauce, minced fine

Juice of 1 large orange

2 tablespoons (30 ml) chopped fresh
  cilantro leaves

- To make mayonnaise, place all ingredients into a medium bowl and whisk until smooth. Keep refrigerated.

- Cut potatoes into 1/4 inch (6 mm) wedges. Place the potatoes, oil and lime juice in a baggie and toss to coat.

- In a small bowl combine the salt, cumin and black pepper; set aside.

- Preheat barbecue to medium heat: 350F (176C). Oil grill.

- Remove potatoes from baggie and place on grill over direct heat. Grill 6–8 minutes per side or until tender and golden brown.

- Remove from grill and sprinkle with seasoning mix.

- Serve hot with Chipotle mayonnaise.

SPINACH SALAD WITH BACON, CASHEWS AND APPLES

Pancetta is more salty and oily than regular bacon (that's a good thing, by the way). You crisp it up by laying slices on a parchment paper-lined baking sheet and sticking it on the BBQ over indirect heat at about 350F (175C) till crisp. Make the dressing first and slice the apple up last, then add the dressing to the salad right away so the apple doesn't discolour. Serves 6

5 cups (1.2 L) spinach leaves

1 cup (250 ml) crumbled freshly cooked bacon or whole pancetta, crisped up

1/2 cup (125 ml) toasted cashews coarsely chopped

2 sweet crisp apples like Gala or Granny Smith sliced into matchsticks, skin on

1/2 cup (125 ml) red onion, sliced thin

1 cup (250 ml) bean sprouts, washed and dried

Vinaigrette:

1 shallot, minced fine

2 tablespoons (30 ml) red wine vinegar

1 tablespoon (15 ml) fresh lemon juice

2 teaspoons (10 ml) Dijon mustard

1/3 cup (83 ml) olive oil

Salt and pepper to taste

- To make the dressing place all ingredients in a small Mason jar and shake until combined.

- Place all fresh ingredients into a bowl and toss. Add pancetta, pour dressing over and toss again to evenly coat.

SUMMER ASIAN PASTA SALAD

There's nothing better than a chilled pasta salad on a warm summer day. It's perfect with grilled pork tenderloin. And you can chop up the leftover pork and add it to the leftover salad and voila – tomorrow's lunch ready to go.

Yield: 6 servings

1 lb (454g) package dried penne noodles

1 tablespoon (15 ml) sesame oil

1/3 cup (85 ml) teriyaki sauce

2–3 teaspoons (10-15 ml) Thai sweet
   chili sauce

Juice of 1 lemon

1 red bell pepper, cored and sliced thin

1 yellow pepper, cored and sliced thin

1/4 cup (60 ml) fresh chopped cilantro leaves

4 green onions, sliced thin

1/4 cup (60 ml) chopped cashews

- Cook pasta in a large pot of boiling salted water for 8–10 minutes or until pasta is el dente (soft yet has a firm texture). Drain pasta and cool.

- In a small bowl, whisk together sesame oil, teriyaki sauce, lemon juice and the Thai chili sauce. Whisk until evenly blended.

- Pour dressing over noodles. Add the fresh peppers, cilantro, green onion and chopped cashews. Mix just to combine.

STRAWBERRY MINT SOUP

This is almost like dessert. Here's what you do next time you have a BBQ dinner party: serve a little shot glass full of this soup as a palate cleanser between courses. Very nice. Yield: 6 bowls

4 cups (1 L) fresh strawberries, hulled

2 cups (500 ml) water

1 cup (250 ml) freshly squeezed orange juice

3 tablespoons (45 ml) chopped ginger

4 stalks fresh lemongrass, tough outer leaves
  removed, inner stalks lightly smashed
  and sliced thin

2 tablespoons (30 ml) rice wine vinegar

1 cup (250 ml) mint leaves, roughly chopped

3/4 cup (190 ml) sugar or more to taste

- Place water, orange juice, ginger, lemongrass, sugar and rice wine vinegar into a large saucepan. Bring mixture to a boil. Reduce heat and simmer for 5 minutes.

- Remove from heat, strain the mixture over a bowl. Stir in the strawberries and cool.

- Place the now cooled mixture in a blender along with the mint leaves and blend until smooth. Adjust sweetness if necessary.

- Chill 1 hour before serving.

SWEET AND SPICY BLACK BEAN SALAD

Black beans are delicious *and* good for you. Why don't we eat more beans?
They're great in this salad which pairs nicely with any grilled fish or chicken.

Serves 6–8

3 cups (750 ml) canned black beans
  drained and rinsed

1 1/2 cups (375 ml) freshly roasted corn
  kernels (see page 200)

3 scallions, thinly sliced, white and green parts

1/2 cup (125 ml) cilantro, roughly chopped

1/2 red bell pepper cut into 1/4-inch dice

1/2 yellow pepper cut into 1/4-inch dice

1/2 red onion cut into medium dice

1 whole avocado peeled, pitted and diced

Dressing:

Juice of 2 limes

1/2 cup (125 ml) canola oil

1 teaspoon (5 ml) chili powder

1 teaspoon (5 ml) ground cumin

Salt and pepper to taste

Optional garnish: lime wedges

- In a large bowl combine all salad ingredients excluding the avocado.

- To make the dressing, combine all ingredients in a small Mason jar. Shake vigorously until evenly mixed. Season with salt and pepper.

- Pour the dressing over the salad and toss to coat and refrigerate for 1 hour to chill.

- Right before serving add the avocado and gently toss the salad.

- Serve with lime wedges.

WATERMELON FETA AND BLACK OLIVE SALAD

I love the way all the flavours and textures play off of each other in this salad. Prepare the salad just before eating so the basil and mint don't go limp and the watermelon doesn't go mushy. Put the salad in the fridge to chill before serving. Serves 6–8

1/4 cup (60 ml) thinly sliced red onion

1 tablespoon (15 ml) fresh lime juice

1 cup (250 ml) crumbled feta cheese

1/2 cup (125 ml) fresh mint leaves, torn

1/4 cup (60 ml) fresh basil leaves, torn

2 tablespoons (30 ml) good quality olive oil

1/2 cup (125 ml) pitted Kalamata black olives

3 lb (1.36 kg) seedless watermelon

Good grind of fresh black pepper to taste

- Cut watermelon into bite-sized pieces and place in a large bowl. Tear and add the fresh mint and basil.

- Add the red onion, fresh lime juice and olive oil.

- Toss the salad gently.

- Add the crumbled feta and black olives.

- Finish the salad with a good turn of black pepper

WILD RICE AND ASPARAGUS SALAD

Asparagus is my favourite summer vegetable, and wild rice is not rice at all (it's a grain). They both have sort of a nutty flavour that plays well off the dressing. Try adding some dried cranberries if you'd like. Serves 6–8

2 cups (500 ml) cooked white rice

2 cups (500 ml) cooked wild rice

1 cucumber, seeded and diced into
   bite sized pieces

1 lb (454 g) asparagus

1 tablespoon (15 ml) olive oil

Salt and pepper

Dressing:

2 tablespoons (30 ml) Dijon mustard

1 tablespoon (15 ml) sherry vinegar

1/4 cup (60 ml) olive oil

Salt and pepper to taste

- In a small jar with a tight fitting lid add all dressing ingredients and shake vigorously to combine.

- Cook rice according to package directions. Cool.

- Trim off and discard woody ends of asparagus, toss spears in olive oil and season with salt and pepper.

- Preheat barbecue to high: 475F–500F (246C–260C). Oil grill.

- Place asparagus directly on grates and cook 1–2 minutes while turning or until bright green and slightly charred. Remove from grill and cool.

- Once cool, cut into 1 inch (2.5 cm) pieces.

- Combine the wild and long grain rice, chopped cucumber and grilled asparagus in a large bowl. Pour the dressing over and toss all the ingredients together.

- Season to taste with salt and pepper.

PUMPKIN TAMALES WITH ORANGE GINGER

Tamales may seem daunting at first glance but they are really simple to make. To the basic masa mixture you can add a variety of ingredients such as goat cheese, basil and hot chili peppers. Tamales are served as a side like a baked potato. Yield: 10 tamales

Basic Masa mixture:

3/4 cup (190 ml) fresh corn kernels

1/2 cup (125 ml) medium diced Spanish onion

1 cup (250 ml) chicken stock

3 tablespoons (45 ml) unsalted butter

3 tablespoons (45 ml) shortening

3/4 cup (190 ml) yellow cornmeal

1 teaspoon (5 ml) white sugar

Filling:

1 cup (250 ml) canned pumpkin puree
   (not pie filling)

1/4 cup (60 ml) liquid honey

1 teaspoon (5 ml) ground cinnamon

1/2 teaspoon (2.5 ml) ground nutmeg

1 teaspoon (5 ml) ground cumin

24 cornhusks soaked in cool water for
   2 hours, cleaned and drained

Orange butter:

1/2 cup (125 ml) unsalted butter

1 tablespoon (15 ml) orange zest

Pinch of nutmeg

1 teaspoon (5 ml) grated ginger

Salt and pepper

For the basic tamale:

- Puree corn, onion and stock in a food processor.

- Transfer mixture to a mixing bowl and cut in the butter and shortening.

- Using your fingers, mix in the cornmeal, sugar, salt and pepper and set aside.

For the filling:

- In a separate mixing bowl combine all the filling ingredients.

- Add the pumpkin mixture to the basic tamale mixture, marbling it through the masa.

To make butter:

- Place all ingredients into a food processor and blend until evenly combined.

- Cut a piece of foil approximately 10 inch x 8 inch (25 cm x 20 cm). Spread the butter in a block about 6 inches (15 cm) long and 2 inches (5 cm) thick in the middle of the foil. Roll up and refrigerate 30 minutes.

- Pick out 20 of the best cornhusks. Tear the remaining husks into 1 inch (1.6 cm) strips. These will be used for tying.

- Lay 2 husks flat on a work surface with the tapered ends facing out and broad bases overlapping by 3 inches (5 cm).

- Place about 1/3 cup (83 ml) of the mixture in the centre. Bring the long sides up over the filling, slightly overlapping, and pat down to close. Tie each end of the bundle with a strip of the cornhusk, pushing the filling towards the middle as you tie. Trim the ends.

- Preheat barbecue to 220F (104C) with one burner on and 2 burners off and. Place a drip pan under the grill on the side that is off. Place the tamales over the grates with the drip pan below.

- Allow the tamales to slow cook with lid down for 35–40 minutes. Remove from barbecue.

- To serve, use a knife to make a long cut lengthwise, and place a slice of the butter on top of the hot filling.

GRILLED PIZZA TWO WAYS FOR ADULTS AND KIDS

Two pizza recipes you can do at the same time – simple classic pizza sauce with mozzarella for the kids and a decadent peach and Cambozola pie for the grown ups. Most decent grocery stores sell frozen pizza dough these days. You can also find a local pizza joint (don't bother with the big chains) and ask to buy the dough from them. If you've never had Cambozola cheese before, think creamy brie with a kick. It's excellent on a pizza or after dinner with grapes and port. Yield: 6 mini pizzas

1 lb (454 g) purchased pizza dough

Olive oil for brushing

Flour for dusting

Classic Sauce and Cheese for the Kids

3/4 cup (187 ml) good quality pizza sauce

2 cups (500 ml) shredded mozzarella cheese

Fresh Peach and Cambozola for the Adults

1 1/2 cups (375 ml) fresh summer peaches
    sliced approximately 1/4 inch (6 mm) thick

8 1/4-inch (6-mm) slices of Cambozola cheese

3 tablespoons (45 ml) basil pesto, pre-made

Pepper to taste

- Divide the dough into 6 equal pieces, and roll into rounds approximately 1/4 inch (6 mm) thick on a flour-dusted cutting board.

- Place on an oiled tray and oil the tops using a pastry brush.

- Bring all the toppings with the dough to the barbecue.

- Preheat grill to medium high: 375F (190C). Oil grill.

- Place the pizza skins directly on the grill. Close the lid and grill for 1–2 minutes or until the pizza puffs and has some nice grill marks. Flip over.

- Working quickly, start adding the toppings.

- For half of the pizzas spread 1–2 tablespoons of sauce on the crust leaving a 1/4-inch (6-mm) border. Top with cheese.

- For the remaining 3 pizzas, spread the crust with the pesto, top with the sliced peaches and dot on the Cambozola equally. Sprinkle with fresh pepper.

- Close barbecue lid and cook for 3–4 minutes or until crust is golden brown and cheese is melted.

- With a large hamburger flipper remove pizza. Cool slightly and cut into portions.

GRILLED VEGETABLE PIZZA PANINI SANDWICHES

Your run-of-the-mill panini is made with bread (usually Italian bread called ciabatta) but we go the extra mile on *Road Grill* to bring you the mother of all panini – made with pizza dough. This one is all vegetarian, full of nicely charred veggies and pesto. Great hot off the grill or the next day for lunch if you have leftovers. Yield: 6 sandwiches

2 lb (908 g) store-bought or homemade
    pizza dough

2 tablespoons (30 ml) olive oil

2 tablespoons (30 ml) balsamic vinegar

2 baby eggplant, skin on and sliced into
    1/4 inch (6 mm) rounds

1 green summer zucchini, sliced skin on
    into 1/4 inch (6 mm) rounds

1 yellow pepper, quartered, seeds removed

1 red pepper, quartered, seeds removed

4 portobello mushrooms, cleaned,
    stems removed

1 medium red onion, peeled and quartered
    leaving the root intact

1/4 cup (60 ml) fresh basil, chopped

1 1/2 cups (375 ml) grated asiago cheese

1/4 cup (60 ml) basil pesto, store-bought
    or homemade

Salt and pepper to taste

Olive oil for brushing

All purpose flour for dusting

3 large bricks covered in foil

- Place all the vegetables in a bowl and drizzle with olive oil and balsamic vinegar. Using tongs, toss to coat evenly and season with salt and pepper.

- Preheat barbecue to medium high: 375F (190C). Oil grill.

- Place onion on the grill and cook for 4 minutes per side or until slightly softened and golden brown.

- Place the portobello gill-side up on grill and cook for 3 minutes. Remove when nicely charred and slightly softened. (Do not flip)

- Place peppers on the grill and cook for approximately 1 1/2 minutes per side or until nicely charred yet still slightly firm.

- Zucchini and eggplant will take approximately 1 1/2 minutes per side or until nice char marks are achieved.

- Remove all vegetables and cool.

- Once cool, cut mushrooms, peppers and onions into bite-sized pieces. Place all vegetables in a bowl and toss with the fresh basil.

- On a lightly floured surface divide the dough into 6 equal portions. Using a rolling pin roll the dough out to form 5–6 inch circles, and place them on a large, floured baking tray.

- Preheat barbecue to medium-high direct heat: 375F (190C). Oil grill.

- Place dough directly on well-oiled grill. Cook the dough for 3–4 minutes, with the lid down or until

nice golden char marks are on one side and the dough has puffed. Flip the dough.

- Working quickly, spread the pesto over the dough evenly leaving a 1/2 inch (1.3 cm) border.

- Place the vegetable mixture along one side of dough, sprinkle with cheese. Fold over to make a half moon shape.

- Place a brick covered in foil, or cast iron pan, onto the sandwiches. Cook 3 minutes with the weight or until the cheese is melted and golden char marks are achieved.

- Check bottom of the dough under the brick to ensure it is not over-browning. Remove. Cut into wedges.

GRILLED CORN ON THE COB

This is the basic method, but have fun with seasoning – use Cajun spice instead of salt and pepper. Serves 8

8 cobs of corn, husked

1 tablespoon (15 ml) melted butter

Salt and pepper

Oil for brushing

- Preheat barbecue to medium high: 375F (190C). Oil grill.

- Brush the cobs with melted butter.

- Season with salt and pepper.

- Place the corn directly on grill.

- Cook while turning until golden brown char marks are achieved, about 4 minutes.

Slice kernels off the cooled cobs to use in a variety of recipes.

DESSERTS

It's always a good idea to keep your BBQ grill clean, and
especially so if you plan to barbecue dessert. Trust me,
you don't want your grilled plums to taste like salmon!

GRILLED PLUMS WITH LIME MASCARPONE

Grilled fruit tends to be the go-to BBQ dessert but most people don't think about grilling plums. Dipping the halved flesh in sugar gives them a caramel crust. Mascarpone is a creamy sweet Italian cheese that works perfectly with the tartness of the lime juice. Put them together with a reduced port sauce and you've got a great grown-up dessert. Serves 6

12 ripe ruby plums

3 tablespoons (45 ml) white
  granulated sugar

Sauce:

1 cup (250 ml) ruby red port

3 tablespoons (45 ml) sugar

1 cinnamon stick

1 vanilla bean, scraped

2 teaspoons roughly chopped ginger

Zest of 1 orange

Lime mascarpone cream:

1 cup (250 ml) Italian mascarpone cheese

1/2 cup (125 ml) 35% whipping cream

2–3 tablespoons (30–45 ml) icing sugar

Zest and juice of 1 lime

- To make sauce, combine all the sauce ingredients in a small saucepan set over medium-low heat. Simmer sauce until slightly thickened.

- Remove from heat, strain the liquid and chill.

- Whip cream with the icing sugar until soft peaks form.

- In a separate bowl combine the mascarpone cheese, lime juice and zest.

- Fold in the whipped cream and stir just to combine.

- Chill cream for 30 minutes.

- Preheat barbecue to medium high: 375F (190C). Oil grill.

- Slice plums in half and remove the pit. Dip the flesh side in the sugar.

- Place on the grill sugar-side down and grill until the sugar is caramelized and golden char marks are achieved. Flip and cook the plums for 2 minutes or until the plum is slightly softened. Remove from grill.

- Place 2 grilled plums on each plate, drizzle with sauce and top with a tablespoon of the cream.

GRILLED SUGAR CINNAMON DONUTS

And you thought all BBQ desserts were grilled fruit of some sort. This is a fun and easy recipe and the kids can pitch in, too. They get to wrap the bricks in tin foil and smoosh the donuts down once they've hit the grill. Careful! Yield: 6 donuts

6 store-bought plain cake donuts

2 tablespoons (30 ml) melted butter

3 tablespoons (30 ml) white sugar

1 1/2 teaspoons (7.5 ml) ground cinnamon

3 heavy bricks wrapped in foil.

1 cup (250 ml) crème fraiche

- Preheat barbecue to medium: (350F) (175C). Oil grill.

- Mix together the cinnamon and sugar in a small bowl; transfer to a small plate.

- Brush both sides of each donut with melted butter. Dip each side of the donut in the cinnamon sugar mixture.

- Place each donut on the grill and top with the foil-covered bricks to weight them down. Cook for 2 minutes per side or until the sugar is caramelized and donuts are crispy and toasted.

- Remove from grill serve with coffee or a dollop of crème fraiche.

KETTLE CORN

We wanted to try something a bit different than the usual grilled fruit for a BBQ dessert and came up with kettle corn. It's a sweet and salty snack and you can make it in no time. Yield: 4 cups (1 L)

1/4 cup (60 ml) vegetable oil

1/4 cup (60 ml) white sugar

1/2 cup (125 ml) popcorn

Salt to taste

- Preheat barbecue to high – as high as she goes.

- Set a cast iron pot on the barbecue with the lid closed for 10 minutes to preheat. (Alternately, if you have a side burner place the pan over high heat for 3 minutes and continue with recipe.)

- Place oil in pan and heat 2 minutes. Add 3 kernels of corn to the pan. Wait for the kernels to pop then add rest of the popcorn.

- Wait for the sizzle of the corn and pour in the sugar. Using a wooden spoon stir to evenly mix the corn and the sugar. Place the lid on and give a good shake of the pan, using barbecue gloves or a dry towel.

- Allow popcorn to cook while constantly shaking for 4 minutes. Once popping has subsided, remove from barbecue or side burner and pour onto a baking tray.

- While still super-hot sprinkle with salt so it sticks to the corn.

MELON BALL SALAD

You can serve this one either as a first course or as dessert really, just make sure it's cold. Mint, lime juice and honey are all you need besides some nice fresh, juicy melons. Serves 6–8

1 large ripe cantaloupe

1 ripe honeydew melon

1 small seedless watermelon or 1/2 a large

1/2 cup (125 ml) fresh mint leaves, chiffonade

Juice of 2 limes

1/4 cup (60 ml) liquid honey

Special tools: melon baller

- In a small bowl mix together the lime juice, honey and chiffonade of mint.

- Cut the honeydew, watermelon and cantaloupe in half. Remove and discard seeds.

- Using a melon baler, make melon balls and place in a large bowl.

- Drizzle with dressing.

PINEAPPLE BANANA GRILLED FRUIT STICKS WITH VANILLA BUTTER

Resist the urge to use that bottled artificial vanilla stuff. Pop for the real vanilla bean as it really makes this dessert. This is so easy to make and so delicious. No one can resist it. Yield: 8 skewers

3 bananas, peeled and cut into 1 inch
   (2.5 cm) rounds
1 whole pineapple peeled and cut into
   1 inch (2.5 cm) squares
2 tablespoons (30 ml) melted unsalted butter
8 bamboo skewers soaked in cool water
   for 30 minutes

Glaze:
1 vanilla bean, scraped
1/3 cup (83 ml) brown sugar
2 tablespoons (30 ml) unsalted butter

Serving suggestion:
1 cup (250 ml) vanilla yogurt

- To make the glaze, place all ingredients in a small saucepan over medium-low heat and stir frequently for 5–10 minutes or until slightly thickened and caramelized.

- Cut all the fruit into even 1 inch (2.5 cm) pieces. Thread fruit onto skewers, alternating the fruits.

- Brush fruit with melted butter and set skewers on a tray.

- Preheat barbecue to medium high: 375F (190C). Oil grill.

- Place fruit on direct heat and cook 2 minutes per side or until slightly caramelized and golden brown.

- In the last minute of cooking, brush with the glaze. Remove from grill and brush with remaining glaze.

- Serve hot with store-bought vanilla yogurt.

RUBS & MARINADES
GLAZES & SAUCES
BUTTERS & DIPS
DRESSINGS
SALSAS & CHUTNEYS

We pulled all the sauces, rubs, glazes, butters, chutneys and salsas from the **Road Grill** recipes and compiled them in one chapter. Plus, we've added some extras we're fond of using.

Basically a "rub" is any combination of dry granular ingredients "rubbed" onto the flesh of whatever you will be BBQing. Rubbing creates micro-tears (or teeny tiny pockets if you will), thereby insinuating the rub flavours into the flesh. It also creates a nice coating that crisps up when grilled.

Marinades are always liquid (although they certainly can include dry ingredients). Marinades serve two purposes. They soak into whatever you will be barbecuing and infuse it with flavour. In certain instances, marinades (especially ones with an acid component) also serve to tenderize tougher cuts by breaking down the connective tissues.

Either way, rubs and marinades add flavour. As always, we encourage you to mess with the ingredients and quantities to create your own special concoction.

I know we've covered this already but it's worth repeating. Make sure you do not leave your fish or shellfish in a marinade that has an acidic component (like wine or vinegar or fruit juice) longer than it says in the recipe. Acid "cooks" the fish or shellfish (that's how you make seviche) making it tough and rubbery long before it hits the grill.

There are some great chutneys and salsas included here. Sometimes you just want a nice simple piece of grilled fish or chicken without any muss or fuss. That's when the flavor pop comes from a salsa or a chutney.

Sure, there are plenty of good store-bought salsas and chutneys out there. But check the ingredients. A lot of them include tons of sugar or shelf stabilizers. Try making your own – they are the simplest things to make. They'll keep in the fridge for at least a week or two, depending on the ingredients.

Rubs

BLACKENING SPICE

Yield: Approximately 1/4 cup (75 ml) plus
1 tablespoon (15 ml)

> 2 tablespoons (30 ml) paprika
>
> 2 teaspoons (10 ml) dried thyme leaves
>
> 2 teaspoons (10 ml) ground cayenne
>
> 1 teaspoon (5 ml) ground white pepper
>
> 2 teaspoons (10 ml) garlic powder
>
> 2 teaspoon (10 ml) onion powder

- Place all ingredients in a bowl and mix evenly.
- Store in an airtight container.

CHINESE 5-SPICE RUB

Yield: Approximately 1/2 cup (125 ml)

> 4 teaspoons (20 ml) Chinese five-spice powder
>
> 2 tablespoons (30 ml) salt
>
> 1 tablespoon (15 ml) freshly ground
> black pepper
>
> 2 tablespoons (30 ml) lightly packed
> brown sugar
>
> 2 teaspoons (10 ml) chili flakes

- In a small bowl, combine all ingredients and mix.
- Store in an airtight container.

BRICK CHICKEN RUB

Yield: Approximately 1/4 cup (60 ml)

> 2 teaspoons (10 ml) ground cumin
>
> 1 teaspoon (5 ml) ground coriander
>
> 1 teaspoon (5 ml) cinnamon
>
> 1 teaspoon (5 ml) red chili pepper flakes
>
> 1 teaspoon (5 ml) salt
>
> 1 teaspoon (5 ml) fresh ground pepper

- Place all ingredients in a bowl and mix evenly.
- Store in an airtight container.

CHIPOTLE STEAK RUB

Yield: 1/2 cup (125 ml)

> 3 dried chipotle peppers
>
> 3 tablespoons (45 ml) black peppercorns
>
> 2 tablespoons (30 ml) dried oregano
>
> 1 tablespoon (15 ml) dried cilantro leaves
>
> 1 dried bay leaf
>
> 1 teaspoon (5 ml) cumin seeds
>
> 1 teaspoon (5 ml) onion powder
>
> 1 teaspoon (5 ml) brown sugar
>
> 1 teaspoon (5 ml) ground dry orange peel

- Place all ingredients in a spice mill or coffee grinder.
- Grind using on and off turns until fine.
- Store in an airtight container for up to 2 months.

CITRUS HERBAL TEA RUB

Yield: Approximately 2 cups (500 ml)

1/2 cup (125 ml) green tea leaves

1/4 cup (60 ml) dried peppermint or mint

*1/2 cup (125 ml) lemon grass powder
  or flakes*

1 tablespoon (15 ml) kosher salt

*1/4 cup (60 ml) dried orange zest
  see note**

1/4 cup (60 ml) dried lime zest

2 tablespoons (30 ml) dried lemon zest

2 tablespoons (30 ml) ground ginger

- Combine all ingredients in a medium bowl.

- Use immediately or store in an airtight container.

Note: this recipe calls for dried orange, lemon and lime zest. You can find these in most Asian food stores, but they are easy to make and have lots of uses. Zest the fruit, spread the zests on a baking sheet, bake for 2 hours at 200F (95C) or until zests are dried. Store in a sealed container in the refrigerator.

CLASSIC ALL PURPOSE RUB

Yield: Approximately 3/4 cup (190 ml)

1/4 cup (60 ml) brown sugar

3 tablespoons (45 ml) sweet paprika

1 tablespoons (15 ml) kosher salt

2 teaspoons (10 ml) garlic powder

2 teaspoons (10 ml) onion powder

2 teaspoons (10 ml) ground cinnamon

1 teaspoon (5 ml) ground coriander

1 teaspoon (5 ml) cayenne pepper

2 teaspoons (10 ml) mustard powder

1 teaspoon (5 ml) cracked black pepper

- In a small bowl combine and mix all ingredients.

- Store in an airtight container.

JERK RUB

Yield: Approximately 3/4 cup (190 ml)

2 tablespoons (30 ml) ground coriander

2 tablespoons (30 ml) ground ginger

2 tablespoons (30 ml) lightly packed
brown sugar

1 tablespoon (15 ml) onion powder

1 tablespoon (15 ml) garlic powder

1 tablespoon (15 ml) salt

2 teaspoons (10 ml) ground habanero
or cayenne pepper

2 teaspoons (10 ml) ground black pepper

2 teaspoons (10 ml) dried thyme leaves

1 teaspoon (5 ml) ground cinnamon

1 teaspoon (5 ml) ground allspice

1/2 tsp (2.5 ml) ground cloves

- Place all ingredients in a bowl and mix evenly.
- Store in an airtight container.

LEMON THYME WET RUB

Yield: Approximately 1/3 cup (80 ml)

2 tablespoons (30 ml) olive oil

1 tablespoon (15 ml) fresh ground pepper

1 tablespoon (15 ml) lemon zest

1 tablespoon (15 ml) fresh thyme leaves,
stems removed

Salt to taste

- Mix ingredients together and use immediately or store in an airtight container in the refrigerator.

OOH-LA-LA HORSERADISH RUB

Yield: Approximately 2 1/2 cups (625 ml)

3/4 cup (190 ml) freshly grated
horseradish root

1/2 cup (125 ml) finely chopped garlic

1/4 cup (60 ml) kosher salt

1/4 cup (60 ml) black pepper

1/2 cup (125 ml) olive oil

2 tablespoons (30 ml) ground cumin

1 teaspoon (5 ml) dried oregano

1 teaspoon (5 ml) lemon zest

1 teaspoon (5 ml) lemon juice

1 tablespoon (15 ml) Dijon mustard

1 tablespoon (15 ml) brown sugar

- Place all ingredients into a food processor, process until smooth and evenly combined.
- Place into an airtight container and refrigerate.

SPICY CHILI CRUST

Yield: 1/2 cup (125 ml)

1/4 cup (60 ml) ancho chili powder

1 tablespoon (15 ml) chili flakes

2 teaspoons (10 ml) ground cumin

1 tablespoon (15 ml) freshly ground
    black pepper

1 tablespoon (15 ml) kosher salt

- In a small bowl combine the ingredients.
- Store in an airtight container.

SPICY COFFEE-SPICE RUB
(Great for steaks)

Yield: Approximately 2 cups (500 ml)

1/4 cup (60 ml) ancho chili powder

1/4 cup (60 ml) finely ground espresso beans

2 tablespoons (30 ml) sweet paprika

2 tablespoons (30 ml) dark brown sugar

1 tablespoon (15 ml) mustard powder

1 tablespoon (15 ml) kosher salt

1 tablespoon (15 ml) freshly ground
    black pepper

1 tablespoon (15 ml) ground coriander

2 teaspoons (10 ml) ground ginger

1 tablespoon (15 ml) dried oregano

2 teaspoons (10 ml) ground cayenne

- Combine all ingredients in a bowl.
- Store in an airtight container.

SPICY RIB RUB

Yield: Approximately 3/4 cup (190 ml)

1/4 cup (60 ml) lightly packed brown sugar

2 tablespoons (30 ml) kosher salt

1 teaspoon (5 ml) freshly grated nutmeg

2 teaspoons (10 ml) ground cinnamon

2 teaspoons (10 ml) mustard powder

1 teaspoon (5 ml) dry thyme leaves

2 teaspoons (10 ml) onion powder

2 teaspoons (10 ml) garlic powder

1 teaspoon (5 ml) ground allspice

2 teaspoons (10 ml) dried sage

2 teaspoons (10 ml) dried oregano

- Combine all ingredients in a small bowl.
  Mix to combine flavours evenly.
- Store in an airtight container.

SPICY TEXAS RUB

Yield: 3/4 cup (190 ml)

1/2 cup (125 ml) ancho chili powder
    (or your favourite chili powder)

2 tablespoons (30 ml) sweet paprika

1 tablespoon (15 ml) ground cumin

1 tablespoon (15 ml) mustard powder

1 tablespoon (15 ml) course salt

2 teaspoons (10 ml) ground cayenne pepper

- Combine all ingredients in a small bowl.
  Mix to combine flavours evenly.
- Store in an airtight container.

TURKEY PASTRAMI SPICE MIX

Yield: Approximately 1 1/4 cups (310 ml)

3 tablespoons (45 ml) crushed

  coriander seeds

3 tablespoons (45 ml) cracked pepper

1 1/2 tablespoons (22.5 ml) chopped garlic

1 tablespoon (15 ml) yellow mustard seeds

1/4 cup (60 ml) course salt

1/4 cup (60 ml) brown sugar

2 tablespoons (30 ml) Spanish paprika

2 tablespoons (30 ml) fresh minced ginger

- Place the coriander seeds in a dishtowel and crush with a heavy skillet.

- Combine the cracked seeds with remaining rub ingredients in a small bowl and mix.

WET HERB AND HORSE-RADISH PASTE/RUB

Yield: Approximately 1 cup (250 ml)

1 tablespoon (15 ml) garlic minced

1 tablespoon (15 ml) prepared horseradish

1/2 cup (125 ml) mixed fresh herbs such as

  rosemary, savory, oregano and thyme

3 tablespoons (45 ml) olive oil

Salt and freshly ground pepper to taste

- Place all ingredients into a food processor and pulse on and off until smooth.

- Store in an airtight container in the refrigerator until ready to use.

Marinades

APRICOT DIJON MARINADE

Yield: Approximately 1 cup (250 ml)

> 1/4 cup (60 ml) Dijon mustard
>
> 1/4 cup (75 ml) plus 1 tablespoon (15 ml)
>
> > good quality apricot jam
>
> 1 tablespoon (15 ml) fresh ginger,
>
> > chopped fine
>
> 1/4 cup (60 ml) rice wine vinegar
>
> 1/4 cup (60 ml) olive oil
>
> Salt and pepper to taste

- Combine all ingredients in a small bowl.

BEER AND HERB MARINADE

Yield: 1 1/2 cups (375 ml)

> 1/2 cup (125 ml) olive oil
>
> 2 teaspoons (10 ml) finely chopped garlic
>
> 1 tablespoon (15 ml) fresh rosemary,
>
> > roughly chopped
>
> 1 tablespoon (15 ml) fresh oregano, minced
>
> 1/2 cup (125 ml) dark beer
>
> Pepper to taste

- Whisk together all ingredients.

FLANK STEAK FAJITA MARINADE

Yield: Approximately 1/2 cup (125 ml)

> 1 tablespoon (15 ml) chili powder
>
> 1 teaspoon (5 ml) ground coriander
>
> 1 1/2 teaspoons (7.5 ml) ground cumin
>
> 1/2 teaspoon (2.5 ml) garlic powder
>
> 1/2 teaspoon (2.5 ml) black pepper
>
> 2 limes, zested and juiced
>
> 1/4 cup (60 ml) vegetable oil
>
> Salt and pepper to taste

- Combine all ingredients in a small bowl.

- Store in an airtight container in the refrigerator.

HABANERO MANGO SAUCE/MARINADE FOR SEAFOOD

Yield: Approximately 3 cups (750 ml)

> 3 mangos, peeled, stone removed and
>   roughly chopped
> 2 habanero chilies, seeded and chopped
> 2 green onions, roughly chopped
> 1 clove garlic, chopped fine
> 1 tablespoon (15 ml) finely chopped
>   fresh ginger
> 1/4 cup (60 ml) roughly chopped
>   cilantro leaves
> 1 cup (250 ml) rice wine vinegar
> Juice of 2 limes
> Salt to taste

- Place the habanero, green onion, garlic, ginger and mango in a blender and blend until smooth.

- Turn motor off and add the cilantro and rice wine vinegar.

- Blend using on and off turns until evenly combined.

- Add salt if desired, to taste.

HERB PASTE MARINADE FOR POULTRY

Yield: 3/4 cup (190 ml)

> 1/4 cup (60 ml) fresh rosemary, leaves only
> 1 tablespoon (15 ml) fresh oregano leaves
> 2 tablespoons (30 ml) fresh thyme leaves
> 6–8 cloves of fresh garlic, peeled and
>   roughly chopped
> 2 tablespoons (30 ml) olive oil
> Zest of 1 orange
> Zest of 1 lemon
> 2 teaspoons (10 ml) orange juice
> 2 teaspoons (10 ml) lemon juice
> 1 teaspoon (5 ml) kosher salt
> 1 teaspoon (5 ml) freshly ground
>   black pepper

- Place all ingredients in a food processor and process until well blended.

- Remove and place in an airtight container and refrigerate.

HONEY MUSTARD SAUCE

Yield: Approximately 1 cup (250 ml)

1/2 cup (125 ml) liquid honey

1/4 cup (60 ml) Dijon mustard

1 teaspoon (5 ml) mustard seeds

2 teaspoons (10 ml) chopped garlic

Juice and zest of 1 lemon

2 tablespoons (30 ml) olive oil

Salt and pepper to taste

- In a medium bowl, whisk together all ingredients.

JAMAICAN MARINADE

Yield: Approximately 1 1/2cups (375 ml)

1/2 cup (125 ml) finely chopped green onions

*2 Scotch bonnet chilies or jalapeno peppers,
    seeded and chopped*

1 tablespoon (15 ml) chopped garlic

1 medium onion, diced

1 teaspoon (5 ml) cinnamon

1/2 teaspoon (5 ml) cloves, ground

1 teaspoon (5 ml) dried thyme leaves

1/2 teaspoon (2.5 ml) nutmeg

Splash of soy sauce

2 tablespoons (30 ml) dark rum

1/4 cup (60 ml) fresh lime juice

*2 tablespoons (30 ml) finely chopped
    fresh ginger*

1/2 cup (125 ml) vegetable oil

- Combine all ingredients in a blender and puree
  to a smooth consistency.

LAMB SOUVLAKI MARINADE

Yield: Approximately 3/4 cup (190 ml)

1/4 cup (60 ml) fresh lemon juice

3 tablespoons (45 ml) olive oil

1 1/2 tablespoons (22.5 ml) fresh oregano

1 tablespoon (15 ml) fresh chopped garlic

1/4 cup (60 ml) grated Spanish onion

Pepper to taste

- In a medium bowl combine ingredients and mix well.

LIME CILANTRO MARINADE

Yield: Approximately 1 cup (250 ml)

1/2 cup olive oil (125 ml)

1 tablespoon minced fresh garlic (15 ml)

1/4 cup fresh chopped cilantro leaves (60 ml)

3 limes, zested and juiced

1 teaspoon (5 ml) chili flakes, optional for heat

Pepper to taste

- Combine first five ingredients and add pepper to taste.

LEMON CHICKEN MARINADE

Yield: Approximately 2 1/2 cups (625 ml)

Juice of 4 lemons

1 cup (250 ml) frozen lemonade
from concentrate, defrosted

1 1/2 tablespoons (20 ml) garlic, finely chopped

1/2 cup (125 ml) fresh cilantro or fresh basil

1/2 cup (125 ml) vegetable oil or any
neutral flavoured oil

Salt and pepper to taste

- Combine ingredients in a small bowl to mix.

MINT PESTO

Yield: Approximately 2 cups (500 ml)

1 1/2 cups (375 ml) mint leaves, stems removed

2/3 cup (165 ml) fresh parsley leaves

1/4 cup (60 ml) pine nuts or walnuts

Pinch of red pepper flakes

2 teaspoons (10 ml) chopped garlic

2 teaspoons (10 ml) lemon zest

1 tablespoon (15 ml) fresh lemon juice

1/3 cup (83 ml) olive oil

Salt and pepper to taste.

- In a blender or food processor add all ingredients except the oil. Puree until smooth.

- Gradually add the oil through the feed tube. Puree to an even consistency.

PAPAYA MARINADE

Yield: Approximately 3 cups (750 ml)

  1 tablespoon (15 ml) chopped garlic

  2 cups (500 ml) all natural papaya
    juice, unsweetened

  2 tablespoons (30 ml) fresh lemon juice

  1 teaspoon (5 ml) hot sauce

  1 teaspoon (5 ml) dried red chili flakes

  2 teaspoons (10 ml) dried oregano

  2 teaspoons (10 ml) fish sauce

  1/2 cup (125 ml) Spanish onion, diced fine

  1/4 cup (60 ml) olive oil

  Pepper to taste

- In a medium sized bowl whisk together all ingredients until evenly combined.

POMEGRANATE MOLASSES GLAZE AND MARINADE

Yield: Approximately 1 1/2 cups

  1 cup (250 ml) pomegranate juice

  2 tablespoons (30 ml) molasses

  2 teaspoons (10 ml) finely chopped fresh garlic

  1 medium red onion, finely diced

  2 tablespoons (30 ml) fresh mint,
    roughly chopped

  2 teaspoons (10 ml) brown sugar

  1 teaspoon (5 ml) ground cardamom

  2 tablespoons (30 ml) lemon zest

  2 tablespoons (30 ml) fresh lemon juice

  Salt and pepper to taste

- Warm all ingredients in a small saucepan set over medium heat.

- Bring the mixture to a gentle simmer while stirring.

- Reduce heat and simmer until the liquid has thickened slightly, about 5 minutes.

- Remove from heat and cool completely.

SPICY CHICKEN MARINADE

Yield: Approximately 2 cups (500 ml)

> 1/2 cup (125 ml) olive oil
>
> 1/4 cup (60 ml) fresh lemon juice
>
> 1/4 cup (60 ml) fresh orange juice
>
> 1/4 cup (60 ml) red wine vinegar
>
> 2–3 tablespoons (30–45 ml) Piri Piri or
> your favourite hot pepper sauce
>
> 2 teaspoons (10 ml) paprika
>
> 1/2 teaspoon (2.5 ml) ground cumin
>
> 2 tablespoons (30 ml) chopped fresh
> parsley, leaves only
>
> 2 teaspoons (10 ml) finely chopped
> fresh ginger
>
> 2 teaspoons (10 ml) chopped fresh thyme,
> stems removed
>
> 1 tablespoon (15 ml) chopped fresh garlic

- Place all ingredients in a medium sized bowl and whisk until combined.

TANDOORI MARINADE

Yield: Approximately 1 1/2 cups (375 ml)

> Juice of 1 lemon
>
> 2 teaspoons (10 ml) ground black pepper
>
> 2 cloves of garlic minced
>
> 1 tablespoon (15 ml) freshly grated ginger
>
> 2 teaspoons (10 ml) ground coriander
>
> 1 teaspoon (5 ml) garam masala spice mix
>
> 1 teaspoon (5 ml) ground cayenne
>
> 1 teaspoon (5 ml) ground turmeric
>
> 2 teaspoons (10 ml) hot curry paste
>
> 1 cup (250 ml) plain yogurt
>
> Salt and pepper to taste

- In a medium bowl mix together all ingredients until well combined.

VERDE SAUCE/ MARINADE

Yield: Approximately 2 cups (500 ml)

Juice and zest of 2 lemons

1 cup (250 ml) lightly packed fresh basil, stems removed

1/2 cup (125 ml) fresh mint leaves, stems removed

2 tablespoons (30 ml) fresh oregano leaves, stems removed

1 cup (250 ml) Italian flat leaf parsley, stems removed

4 cloves garlic

2 tablespoons (30 ml) Dijon mustard

2 tablespoons (30 ml) capers, drained

4 anchovy fillets

1/2 cup (125 ml) olive oil

Cracked pepper and salt to taste

- Put the garlic in blender and pulse; add the remaining ingredients and puree until smooth.
- Season to taste with salt and pepper.

WHITE WINE LEMON TARRAGON MARINADE FOR VEAL

Yield: Approximately 1 1/2 cups (750 ml)

1 cup (250 ml) white wine

1/4 cup (60 ml) olive oil

Zest of 2 lemons

2 sprigs fresh tarragon

1/4 cup (60 ml) white onion, chopped fine

1 teaspoon (5 ml) finely chopped garlic

- Place all ingredients for the marinade in a small bowl and whisk until evenly combined.

YOGURT MARINADE FOR SEAFOOD

Yield: Approximately 1 1/4 cups (310 ml)

1 cup (250 ml) whole fat plain yogurt

2 tablespoons (30 ml) fresh horseradish puree

2 tablespoons (30 ml) fresh basil leaves, roughly chopped

1 tablespoon (15 ml) fresh lemon zest

1 tablespoon (15 ml) granulated white sugar

Salt and pepper to taste

- Place all ingredients for the marinade in a medium bowl and whisk until evenly combined.

Glazes & Sauces

ANOTHER CLASSIC BBQ SAUCE

Yield: Approximately 3 cups (750 ml)

2 tablespoons (30 ml) vegetable oil

1 tablespoon (15 ml) chopped garlic

1 cup (250 ml) yellow onion, finely chopped

2 teaspoons (10 ml) chili powder

2 teaspoons (10 ml) mustard powder

1 teaspoon (5 ml) Spanish paprika

Pinch of cayenne

2 cups (500 ml) crushed tomatoes

1 cup (250 ml) ginger beer

1/4 cup (60 ml) molasses

3 tablespoons (45 ml) Worcestershire sauce

3 tablespoons (45 ml) cider vinegar

- Place oil in a large skillet set over medium heat, add the onion and garlic and sauté until onion is translucent.

- Add all the remaining ingredients and reduce the heat to low. Simmer for 25 minutes, stirring occasionally.

- Remove from heat and cool.

ASIAN CHICKEN GLAZE

Yield: 1 1/4 cup (310 ml)

2 tablespoons (30 ml) peanut oil

2 tablespoons (30 ml) grated ginger

1 1/2 tablespoons (23 ml) chopped garlic

1/4 cup (60 ml) soy sauce

3/4 cup (190 ml) good quality honey

Juice of 2 lemons

1 teaspoon (5 ml) freshly ground black pepper

- Heat the oil in a medium saucepan set over medium-high. Add the ginger and garlic and cook while stirring until soft, without browning.

- Stir in the soy sauce, lemon juice and honey.

- Remove from heat; add black pepper and cool.

CONCORD GRAPE SAUCE

Yield: 2 cups (500 ml)

2 lb (908 g) concord grapes, stems removed

2 sprigs fresh thyme

2 teaspoons (10 ml) whole black peppercorns

2 star anise, whole

2 cinnamon sticks, each 4 inches (10 cm) long

2 cups (500 ml) unsweetened white grape juice

Salt

- In a saucepan set over medium heat add all the sauce ingredients. Bring to a boil, reduce heat to low and simmer 20 minutes.

- Strain sauce into bowl, season with salt to taste.

CURRIED CORN SAUCE

Yield: 2 1/2 cups (625 ml)

>   2 tablespoons (30 ml) unsalted butter
>   1/2 cup (125 ml) medium diced Spanish onion
>   1 teaspoon (5 ml) finely chopped garlic
>   1 1/2 teaspoon (7.5 ml) grated fresh ginger
>   1/2 medium green apple, peeled,
>   cored and diced
>   1 1/2 tablespoons (23 ml) madras curry paste
>   1/2 cup (125 ml) low sodium chicken stock
>   1 1/2 cups (375 ml) coconut milk
>   1 cup (250 ml) fresh corn kernels
>   1/4 cup (60 ml) fresh cilantro leaves,
>   roughly chopped

- In a medium saucepan set over medium heat add coconut milk and bring to a boil. Reduce heat to low, add curry paste and simmer for 10 minutes.

- In a large sauté pan set over medium heat, add the butter to melt and add the onions, garlic, ginger and apple. Cook while stirring until onion is translucent and fragrant.

- Deglaze pan with the chicken stock and cook a further 1–2 minutes until reduced by half. Add the coconut curry mixture, reduce heat to low and simmer for 3–4 minutes.

- Add the corn to the sauce and cook just to warm the kernels, about 1 minute.

GINGER PLUM SAUCE

Yield: 1 1/2 cups (375 ml)

>   3/4 cup (180 ml) good quality plum jam
>   2 tablespoons (30 ml) fresh lime juice
>   1 tablespoon (15 ml) rice wine vinegar
>   2 teaspoons (10 ml) minced ginger
>   1 tablespoon (15 ml) honey
>   1 teaspoon (5 ml) finely chopped garlic
>   3 tablespoons (45 ml) sesame seeds,
>   lightly toasted

- Combine all the ingredients in a small pot over low heat. Bring the sauce to a simmer for 5 minutes.

HABANERO MAPLE GLAZE AND SAUCE

This can be used as a great dipping sauce or marinade for seafood or chicken. Yield: 2 1/2 cups (625 ml)

3 mangos, peeled, stone removed and
    roughly chopped
2 habanero chilies, seeded and chopped
2 green onions, roughly chopped
1 clove garlic, chopped fine
1 tablespoon (15 ml) finely chopped
    fresh ginger
1/4 cup (60 ml) roughly chopped cilantro leaves
1 cup (250 ml) rice wine vinegar
Juice of 2 limes
Salt to taste

- Place the habanero, green onion, garlic, ginger and mango in a blender and puree until smooth. Turn motor off and add cilantro and rice wine vinegar.

- Pulse on and off until evenly combined.

- Add salt to taste.

HAWAIIAN FRUIT BBQ SAUCE

Yield: 5 cups (1250 ml)

1 lb (454 g) fresh pitted apricot halves
1 lb (454 g) fresh pitted peaches, sliced thin
1 medium can crushed pineapple
1/2 cup (125 ml) applesauce
1 cup (250 ml) white vinegar
1 teaspoon (5 ml) hot sauce
3 tablespoons (45 ml) tomato paste
1 cup (250 ml) firmly packed golden
    brown sugar
2 teaspoons (10 ml) mustard powder
1/2 cup (125 ml) unsalted butter
Juice of 2 limes
Salt and pepper to taste

- Melt butter in a large skillet set over medium heat. Add the peaches and apricots and sauté for 3–4 minutes until nicely caramelized.

- Add remaining ingredients except the lime juice. Stir to combine and reduce heat to low.

- Simmer for 30 minutes or until the mixture is thickened and coats the back of a spoon.

- Allow to cool, season to taste with salt and pepper and add the lime juice.

- Puree in a blender until smooth and strain.

HUNAN BBQ SAUCE

Yield: 2.5 cups (625 ml)

2 cups (500 ml) hoisin sauce

Juice of 3 oranges

2 tablespoons (30 ml) grated ginger

1 1/2 tablespoons (22.5 ml) chopped garlic

1/4 cup (60 ml) dry sherry

2 tablespoons (30 ml) sesame seeds

- Place the hoisin sauce in a medium bowl; add remaining ingredients and stir the mixture to combine.

MAPLE LEMON MARINADE OR SAUCE

Yield: 1 cup (250 ml)

2 tablespoons (30 ml) lemon zest

1/2 cup (125 ml) lemon juice

1/3 cup (85 ml) pure maple syrup

2 tablespoons (60 ml) fresh grated ginger

3 tablespoons (45 ml) bourbon whisky

2 tablespoons (30 ml) fresh mint, chopped fine

Salt and pepper to taste

- Combine all ingredients in a small bowl and whisk.

LIME HOISIN SAUCE

Yield: 3 cups (750 ml)

1/2 cup (125 ml) grape seed oil

2 tablespoons (30 ml) minced garlic

1 tablespoon (15 ml) fresh minced ginger

2 cups (500 ml) hoisin sauce

1/2 cup (125 ml) fresh lime juice

- Mix all ingredients together just to combine.

MOP AND SAUCE FOR BEEF BRISKET

Yield: 2 1/2 cups (625 ml)

1 1/2 cups (375 ml) beef stock

3/4 cup (180 ml) ketchup

Juice of 1 fresh lemon

1/2 tablespoon (7.5 ml) chili powder

1/2 tablespoon (7.5 ml) garlic powder

1/2 tablespoon (7.5 ml) onion powder

1 teaspoon (5 ml) celery salt

- Combine all ingredients in a saucepan set over medium-low heat and cook for 20 minutes.

MUSTARD GLAZE

Yield: Approximately 1 cup (250 ml)

1/4 cup (60 ml) olive oil

Salt and pepper

1/4 cup (60 ml) Dijon mustard

1/4 cup (60 ml) good quality liquid honey

*1 tablespoon (15 ml) fresh summer
    savory, roughly chopped*

1 teaspoon (5 ml) Worcestershire sauce

- Whisk ingredients together in a medium bowl.

ORANGE MANGO GLAZE

Yield: 1 1/2 cups (375 ml)

1 tablespoon (15 ml) unsalted butter

*2 large, ripe mangos, peeled and
    roughly chopped*

1 small red onion cut into 1/4 inch (6 mm) dice

1 jalapeno, seeded and diced

2 teaspoons (10 ml) minced fresh ginger

*1 tablespoon (15 ml) Sambal or your
    favourite hot sauce*

Juice of 3–4 limes

*1 tablespoon (15 ml) frozen orange
    juice concentrate*

Salt and pepper to taste

- Melt butter in a large skillet set over medium-high heat. Add the ginger, onion, jalapeno and mango.

- Cook while stirring for 4 minutes or until onion is translucent and mango is very tender. Remove from heat, add the hot sauce, lime juice and orange juice concentrate. Cool slightly; place all ingredients in a blender and puree until smooth.

- Remove from blender, strain into a bowl and season with salt and pepper.

PEANUT DIPPING SAUCE

Yield: Approximately 1 1/2 cups (375 ml)

2 tablespoons (15 ml) peanut oil

1/2 cup (125 ml) fine diced white onion

2 garlic cloves minced

1 1/2 teaspoons (7.5 ml) chili paste

1/2 teaspoon (2.5 ml) curry powder

2 teaspoons (10 ml) kosher salt

1/4 cup (60 ml) smooth, all natural peanut butter

1/4 cup (60 ml) coconut milk

2 teaspoons (10 ml) rice wine vinegar

2 tablespoons (30 ml) brown sugar

1/4 cup (60 ml) roasted unsalted peanuts, coarsely chopped

1/4 cup (60 ml) boiling water

- Heat oil in a medium skillet over medium heat. Add the onions and garlic and cook until translucent, about 3 minutes.

- Add the chili paste, curry powder and stir to combine. Stir in the peanut butter, coconut milk, rice vinegar, brown sugar and 2 tablespoons of the warm water. Let simmer for 1–2 minutes or until the peanut butter dissolves.

- Add 2 tablespoons (30 ml) of the peanuts to the sauce and transfer to a blender.

- Blend until smooth, adding 2–4 tablespoons of boiling water to help the sauce emulsify. Transfer to a bowl and garnish with remaining peanuts.

PORT SAUCE FOR GRILLED FRUITS

Yield: Approximately 1 cup (250 ml)

1 cup (250 ml) ruby red port

3 tablespoons (45 ml) sugar

1 cinnamon stick

1 vanilla bean, scraped

2 teaspoons roughly chopped ginger

Zest of 1 orange

- In a small saucepan set over medium low heat add all the sauce ingredients. Simmer sauce until slightly thickened.

- Remove from heat, strain into a bowl and chill.

RED PEPPER PESTO

Yield: Approximately 1 cup (250 ml)

1 large red bell pepper

1 garlic clove, minced fine

2 tablespoons (30 ml) olive oil

1/2 teaspoon (2.5 ml) balsamic vinegar

1/2 cup (125 ml) grated Parmesan cheese

1/4 cup (60 ml) fresh basil, leaves
  roughly chopped

Salt and pepper to taste

- Preheat barbecue to high: 450F–475F (232C–246C).

- Lightly brush the pepper with oil.

- Grill the pepper turning often until the skin is blackened all over. Remove and place in a paper bag. (This will encourage the skin to come off easily).

- Peel the pepper and remove the seeds and core

- Place the pepper into a food processor with the garlic and puree until smooth. With the processor running, gradually add the olive oil and vinegar.

- Stir in cheese and basil and season with salt and pepper.

SUICIDE HOT SAUCE

Yield: 3 1/2 cups (875 ml)

1/2 cup (125 ml) unseasoned rice vinegar

1/2 cup (125 ml) apple cider vinegar

2 teaspoons (10 ml) ground coriander

1/2 teaspoon (2.5 ml) ground cloves

1/2 teaspoon (2.5 ml) ground allspice berries

1 medium onion diced fine

2 teaspoons (10 ml) garlic minced

1/2 cup (125 ml) lightly packed brown sugar

2 tablespoons (30 ml) blackstrap molasses

2 teaspoons (10 ml) Worcestershire sauce

1/2 bottle dark beer

1/4 cup (60 ml) chipotle chili in adobo
  sauce, minced

1 tablespoon (15 ml) ground chili paste
  (optional for extra heat)

2 cups (500 ml) crushed tomatoes

Salt and pepper

- Combine all ingredients in a saucepan over high heat. Bring to a boil, reduce heat to low and simmer 20 minutes.

- Remove from heat and cool.

SUMMER BING CHERRY SAUCE

Yield: 2 cups (500 ml)

> 2 cups (500 ml) red wine such as a
>   rich Cabernet
>
> 1 whole shallot, diced fine
>
> 1 sprig of fresh rosemary
>
> 1 tablespoon (15 ml) fresh ginger, sliced
>
> 1 tablespoon (15 ml) balsamic vinegar
>
> 2 cups (500 ml) fresh, pitted Bing cherries,
>   sliced
>
> Salt and pepper to taste

- Add the wine, shallot, ginger and rosemary to a medium saucepan. Place over medium heat and bring to a gentle boil.

- Reduce heat to low and simmer until reduced by half.

- Strain the liquid into a bowl using a fine mesh strainer. Add the sliced cherries and balsamic vinegar while wine mixture is still hot.

- Season with salt and pepper to taste.

SAUCY BBQ GLAZE FOR CHICKEN OR RIBS

Yield: 2 1/2 cups (625 ml)

> 2 tablespoons (30 ml) olive oil
>
> 1 medium Spanish onion, diced
>
> 2 tablespoons (30 ml) minced garlic
>
> 2 tablespoons (30 ml) jalapeno pepper,
>   seeded, veins removed and chopped fine
>
> 1 cup (250 ml) tomato paste
>
> 1 cup (250 ml) strong coffee
>
> 1/2 cup (125 ml) Worcestershire sauce
>
> 1/2 cup (125 ml) apple cider vinegar
>
> 1/2 cup (125 ml) lightly packed brown sugar
>
> 1/2 cup (125 ml) fresh apple cider

- Warm olive oil in a medium sauté pan set over high heat for 30 seconds.

- Add the onion and garlic. Cook until the onion is translucent.

- Add remaining sauce ingredients and bring to a boil. Reduce heat to low and simmer 15 minutes. Use immediately or chill.

SWEET SMOKY STICKY BBQ SAUCE

Yield: 2 1/2 cups (625 ml)

1 1/2 cups (375 ml) ketchup

1/4 cup (60 ml) cider vinegar

1/4 cup (60 ml) Worcestershire sauce

1/4 cup (60 ml) brown sugar

2 tablespoons (30 ml) ball park mustard

1 tablespoon (15 ml) hot sauce

1 tablespoon (15 ml) blackening rub
   seasoning (see page 212)

Salt and pepper to taste

- Whisk together all ingredients in a bowl.

SWEET VANILLA GLAZE FOR BBQ FRUIT

Yield: 1/2 cup (125 ml)

1 vanilla bean, scraped

1/2 cup (125 ml) brown sugar

1/4 cup (60 ml) unsalted butter

- Place all ingredients in a small saucepan and cook over medium-low heat, stirring frequently for 5–10 minutes or until slightly thickened and caramelized.

WILD BERRY PORT SAUCE

Yield: 2 cups (500 ml)

1 shallot, sliced thin

2 sprigs of fresh thyme

2 cups (500 ml) ruby port

2 teaspoons (10 ml) finely chopped, fresh,
   peeled ginger

Zest of 1 large orange

2 cups (500 ml) mixed berries (such as
   strawberries, blueberries, raspberries and
   blackberries or whatever is market fresh)

Salt and pepper to taste

- Add the port, thyme, shallot, ginger and orange zest to a medium sized saucepan over medium heat. Bring to a boil then reduce heat to a low simmer.

- Simmer until reduced by half.

- Strain the liquid into a bowl using a fine mesh strainer.

- Add the berries to the hot liquid and stir. This will release some juices into the sauce without ruining the tender berries.

- Season to taste with salt and pepper.

Butters & Dips

BLUE CHEESE ROSEMARY BUTTER

Yield: 1 1/2 cups (375 ml)

1 cup (250 ml) unsalted butter, softened

1/2 cup (125 ml) blue cheese

2 teaspoons (10 ml) freshly ground pepper

2 teaspoons (10 ml) fresh rosemary, chopped

Salt to taste

- Place ingredients into a food processor; pulse until well blended.

- Cut a piece of plastic wrap or foil 10 x 8 inches (25cm x 20cm)

- Spread the butter in a block or cylinder about 6 inches (15cm) long and 2 inches thick in the middle of the wrap and roll up.

- Refrigerate for 30 minutes before slicing.

CHIPOTLE BUTTER

Yield: 1 cup (250 ml)

1/2 cup (125 ml) unsalted butter

1 whole chipotle chili in adobo sauce, minced fine

2 tablespoons (30 ml) cilantro leaves, finely chopped

2 tablespoons (30 ml) fine chopped red onion

- In a food processor, combine the butter, chipotle, onion, cilantro and salt and pepper and process until completely mixed.

- Spread butter in a cylinder about 1 inch (15 cm) in diameter along the long side of a piece of plastic wrap or parchment paper, leaving a 1-inch border. Roll up the butter to make a log. Refrigerate at least 30 minutes.

CHILI LIME AIOLI

Yield: 1 1/4 cups (310 ml)

1 fresh green chili, seeded and finely chopped

2 tablespoons finely chopped cilantro (30 ml)

1 tablespoon fresh lime juice (15 ml)

1 cup (250 ml) store-bought or homemade mayonnaise (see page 243)

Salt and pepper to taste

- Whisk chili, cilantro and lime juice into mayonnaise and season with salt and pepper.

- Keep refrigerated.

CHIPOTLE MAYONNAISE

Yield: 1 1/4 cup (310 ml)

1 cup (250 ml) store-bought or homemade mayonnaise (see page 243)

2 chipotle chilies in adobo sauce, minced fine

Juice of 1 large orange

2 tablespoons (30 ml) chopped fresh cilantro leaves

- Place all ingredients into a medium bowl.

- Whisk until smooth.

- Keep refrigerated.

CILANTRO
CHILI BUTTER

Yield: 1 1/2 cups (375 ml)

> *1 cup (250 ml) unsalted butter, softened*
>
> *1/2 cup (125 ml) cilantro leaves,*
>
> *roughly chopped*
>
> *1 fresh red chili, seeded and chopped*
>
> *1 tablespoon (15 ml) fresh lime juice*
>
> *2 teaspoons (10 ml) salt*
>
> *1 teaspoon (5 ml) freshly ground black pepper*

- Place ingredients into a food processor; pulse until well blended. Place the butter on a large piece of plastic wrap or foil approximately 10 x 8 inches (25cm x 20cm).

- Spread the butter in a block or cylinder about 6 inches (15 cm) long and 2 inches (5 cm) thick in the middle of the plastic wrap or foil and roll up into a cylinder shape.

- Place into refrigerator to set up for 30 minutes.

GARLIC
PARSLEY BUTTER

Yield: 1 1/2 cups (375 ml)

> *1 cup (250 ml) unsalted butter, softened*
>
> *1/2 cup (125 ml) flat leaf parsley chopped*
>
> *2 teaspoons (10 ml) freshly ground pepper*
>
> *Zest and juice of one lemon*
>
> *5 garlic cloves, crushed*
>
> *Salt to taste*

- Place ingredients into a food processor; pulse until well blended. Place the butter on a large piece of plastic wrap or foil approximately 10 x 8 inches (25cm x 20cm).

- Spread the butter in a block or cylinder about 6 inches (15 cm) long and 2 inches (5 cm) thick in the middle of the plastic wrap or foil and roll up into a cylinder shape.

- Place into the refrigerator to set up for 30 minutes.

MAYONNAISE

Yield: 1 1/4 cups (310 ml)

> *2 egg yolks*
>
> *1 teaspoon (5 ml) Dijon mustard*
>
> *1 tablespoon (15 ml) red wine vinegar*
>
> *1/2 teaspoon (2.5 ml) salt*
>
> *Pinch of black pepper*
>
> *2/3 cup (165 ml) canola oil*
>
> *2/3 cup (165 ml) olive oil*

- Make sure that all ingredients are at room temperature before you begin.

- Set a deep bowl on a cloth to prevent it from slipping as you whisk.

- Whisk the egg yolks, mustard, vinegar, salt, and pepper together until thick and creamy.

- Combine the oils in a measuring cup.

- Whisk the oil into the egg yolk mixture a drop at a time, just until it thickens. Add the remaining oil in a thin steady stream, whisking constantly until thick and glossy.

- Adjust seasoning, adding more mustard, vinegar salt and pepper to taste.

- Keeps 3 days in an airtight container in the refrigerator.

Note: If the ingredients are too cold or the oil is added too quickly, the mayonnaise may separate. Don't throw it away. Combine 1 teaspoon (5 ml) vinegar and 1 teaspoon (5 ml) Dijon mustard in a new clean bowl. Whisk into the separated mayonnaise drop by drop until the mixture is emulsified.

ROASTED GARLIC AIOLI

Yield: 1 1/4 cups (310 ml)

> *1 head of garlic*
>
> *1 cup (250 ml) store-bought or homemade
>   mayonnaise (see previous recipe)*
>
> *Zest of one lemon*
>
> *Salt and pepper*

- Slice the top of the garlic, cutting through the cloves. Place cut-side up on a large piece of foil with the sides crimped up.

- Drizzle with olive oil and sprinkle with salt and pepper.

- Roast in a preheated oven at 300F (150C) for 1 hour, until soft.

- Leave to cool completely.

- Squeeze out cloves from the papery skins and mash with a fork until smooth.

- Whisk into mayonnaise and add the lemon zest.

- Keep refrigerated.

Dressings

ZESTY ORANGE BUTTER

Yield: Approximately 1 cup (250 ml)

> 1 cup (250 ml) room temperature
>   unsalted butter
> 1 1/2 tablespoons (22 ml) orange zest
> Salt and pepper

- In a small bowl combine the butter zest, salt and pepper.

- Place ingredients into a food processor; pulse until well blended. Place the butter on a large piece of plastic wrap or foil approximately 10 x 8 inches (25cm x 20cm).

- Spread the butter in a block or cylinder about 6 inches (15 cm) long and 2 inches (5 cm) thick in the middle of the plastic wrap or foil and roll up into a cylinder shape.

- Place into refrigerator to set up for 30 minutes.

Serving Suggestion: Goes great with corn, vegetables and fish dishes. You can also serve this butter in a bowl instead of chilling in plastic wrap.

ASIAN GINGER DRESSING

Yield: 1 cup (250 ml)

> 1/4 cup (60 ml) soy sauce
> 1/4 cup (60 ml) rice wine vinegar
> 3 tablespoons (45 ml) light sesame oil
> 3 tablespoons (45 ml) vegetable oil
> 2 tablespoons (30 ml) white sugar
> 2 tablespoons (30 ml) mirin
> 1 teaspoon (5 ml) garlic minced
> 1 tablespoon (15 ml) fresh minced ginger
> 1 tablespoon (15 ml) fresh lime juice
> 1/4 teaspoon (1.25 ml) cayenne pepper

Optional:

> 2 tablespoons (30 ml) lightly toasted
>   sesame seeds
> 1/4 cup (60 ml) fresh, chopped cilantro leaves

- Whisk ingredients together in a small bowl. Cover and refrigerate for 4 hours to blend flavours.

- Toss with salad of your choice and garnish with fresh chopped cilantro and sesame seeds.

CARIBBEAN MANGO SALSA

Yield: Approximately 3 cups (750 ml)

2 mangos, peeled pitted and cut into
   1/4 inch (6 mm) dice

1/2 pineapple, peeled and cored, cut into
   1/4 inch (6 mm) dice

3 tablespoons (45 ml) red onion, small dice

2 green onions sliced thin

3 tablespoons (45 ml) fresh cilantro leaves,
   chopped roughly

1/2 Thai red chili, chopped fine

Juice of 2 limes

Juice and zest of 1 orange

Salt and pepper

- In a medium bowl combine all the ingredients and mix. Taste, and season with salt and pepper.

FRESH MINT STRAWBERRY SALSA

Yield: Approximately 2.5 cups (625 ml)

2 cups (500 ml) strawberries, cleaned
   and hulled

1/2 cup (125 ml) fresh mint leaves,
   roughly chopped

2 tablespoons (30 ml) red onion, finely diced

2 tablespoons (30 ml) good quality
   balsamic vinegar

Freshly ground pepper and salt to taste

- Smash up the berries until chunky using a fork or dice into small 1/8 inch (3 mm) pieces. Combine with the remaining ingredients and season to taste with salt and pepper.

FRESH SUMMER TOMATO SALSA

Yield: 3–4 cups (750 ml–1 L)

3–4 large ripe tomatoes, chopped small dice

2–3 green onions, sliced thin

1 yellow bell pepper, seeded, diced

1 red bell pepper, seeded, diced

1/2 cup (125 ml) red onion, finely chopped

3 tablespoons (45 ml) chopped cilantro leaves

Juice of 1 lime or 2 depending on
   how juicy they are

1/2 jalapeno chili, seeded, finely diced

Salt and pepper to taste

- In a medium bowl combine all ingredients until evenly combined and season to taste with salt and pepper.

- Cover and refrigerate until chilled.

- This is best served the day it's made.

FUJI APPLE CHUTNEY

Yield: Approximately 2 cups (500 ml)

2 cups (500 ml) Fuji apples peeled, cored
   and cut into 1/4 inch dice

2 tablespoons (30 ml) fresh lemon juice

1 tablespoon (15 ml) vegetable oil

3/4 cup (190 ml) Spanish onion, finely diced

1 tablespoon (15 ml) finely minced ginger

1/2 cup (125 ml) rice wine vinegar

1/2 cup (125 ml) unsweetened apple juice

Salt and pepper to taste

- In a large, non-reactive bowl, toss the apples with the lemon juice.

- Heat the oil in a large saucepan over medium-high for 30 seconds.

- Add the onions and ginger and sauté until onions are translucent and fragrant, 3–4 minutes. Add the apples and cook for 3–4 minutes.

- Add the vinegar and apple juice and cook until liquid is reduced by half.

- Season with salt and pepper to taste and cool to room temperature.

NECTARINE GINGER CHUTNEY

Yield: Approximately 3 cups (750 ml)

> 2 tablespoons (30 ml) vegetable oil
>
> 1/2 cup (125 ml) red onion, finely chopped
>
> 2 teaspoons (10 ml) chopped garlic
>
> 2 tablespoons (30 ml) minced fresh ginger
>
> 1/2 teaspoon (2.5 ml) ground cinnamon
>
> Dash of ground cardamom
>
> Juice of 3 large sweet oranges
>
> Zest of one orange
>
> Juice of 1 lime
>
> 1/4 cup (60ml) rice wine vinegar
>
> 2 tablespoons (30ml) brown sugar
>
> 6 fresh, ripe nectarines pitted and cut
>   into thin slices
>
> 1/4 cup (60ml) fresh mint leaves, chopped
>
> Salt and pepper to taste

- Heat oil in a medium saucepan over high. Add the onion, garlic, ginger, cinnamon and cardamom and sauté until onion is translucent and mixture is fragrant.

- Add the orange juice and zest, lime juice, rice wine vinegar and sugar. Reduce heat to medium, cook until slightly thickened, about 5 minutes.

- Stir in half of the nectarines and cook a further 4 minutes.

- Remove from heat, add the remaining nectarines and fresh mint and season with salt and pepper.

PINEAPPLE SALSA

Yield: 3–4 cups (750 ml-1 L)

> 1/2 pineapple, cored and cut into 1/4 inch
>   (6 mm) cubes
>
> 1 red bell pepper cut into 1/4 inch (6 mm) dice
>
> 2 scallions, sliced thin
>
> 2 tablespoons (30 ml) small dice red onion
>
> 1/2 jalapeno, minced (optional)
>
> 2 tablespoon (30 ml) chopped cilantro leaves
>
> 1 tablespoon (15 ml) fresh lime juice
>
> Salt and pepper

- Combine all ingredients in a medium bowl.

PINEAPPLE TOMATILLO SALSA

Yield: Approximately 3 cups (750 ml)

1 cup (250 ml) fresh ripe pineapple,
  medium dice

3/4 cup (190 ml) chopped tomatillo

3 tablespoons (45 ml) fresh cilantro leaves,
  chopped

1/4 cup (60ml) fresh lime juice

1/2 cup (125 ml) red onion finely diced

3 tablespoons (45 ml) sliced green onion

1/2 cup (125 ml) medium diced red pepper

1/2 jalapeno, seeded and chopped fine

3 tablespoons (45 ml) olive oil

Salt and pepper to taste

- In a medium bowl combine all ingredients and season to taste with salt and pepper.

RED ONION MARMALADE

Goes great with pork, beef, burgers, grilled fish or served cold with cheese. Yield: 1 1/2 cups (375 ml)

1 1/2 lb (680 g) peeled red onions

3 tablespoons (45 ml) unsalted butter

1/4 cup (60 ml) golden brown sugar

1 cup (250 ml) dry red wine

1/4 cup (75 ml) plus 1 tablespoon (15 ml)
  balsamic vinegar

1 tablespoon (15 ml) fresh thyme leaves

Salt to taste

- Slice the onions thinly.

- Melt butter in a large heavy skillet over medium heat. Add onions and sugar and cook until the onions are soft and start to caramelize, about 10 minutes.

- Add the wine and vinegar, bring to a boil and reduce heat to low.

- Add the fresh thyme leaves and simmer for 15 minutes or until the liquid has evaporated and onions have a shiny gloss.

- Remove from heat and season with salt and pepper. Reheat before serving.

SUMMER PEACH SALSA

Yield: 2 cups (500 ml)

4 ripe peaches, peeled, pitted and diced
into 1/8 inch (3 mm) dice
2 tablespoons (30 ml) red onion,
finely chopped
2 scallions, thinly sliced
1/4 cup (60 ml) fresh cilantro leaves,
roughly chopped
1 jalapeno, seeds removed, chopped fine
1/2 a red pepper, seeds removed and
chopped into 1/8 inch (3 mm) dice
Juice of 1 lime
Juice of 1 orange
Salt and pepper to taste

- Combine all ingredients in a medium bowl. Mix well and chill 20 minutes to enhance the flavour before serving.

WARM ROASTED PEACH AND SAGE SALSA

Yield: Approximately 3 cups (750 ml)

6 freestone peaches, cut in half and pitted
1 small red onion, peeled and cut into
1/2 inch (1.3 cm) wedges
1 tablespoon (15 ml) fresh sage, stems
removed, thinly sliced
Juice of 1 large navel orange
Splash of sherry vinegar
Salt and pepper to taste
Olive oil for brushing

- Place the peaches in a bowl and drizzle with olive oil and salt and pepper.

- Cut the onion into 1/2 inch (6 mm) wedges, being sure to keep the root intact as it will hold together well on the barbecue. Drizzle with olive oil and salt and pepper.

- Prepare barbecue for direct grilling at medium high: 375F (190C). Oil grill.

- Place peaches flesh-side down onto grill. Cook for 2–3 minutes until caramelized. Flip and continue to cook on the skin side for 2 minutes.

- Place onions on the grill and cook on each side 2–4 minutes until softened and nice golden char marks are achieved.

- Remove peaches and onions from the grill. Slip the skins off the peaches (they should slide off easily). With a fork, mash the peaches slightly in a bowl.

- Petal off the onion from the root and mix into the peaches. Add the sage, sherry vinegar, orange juice and season with salt and pepper. Serve warm.